MOUNT WHITNEY:

Mountain Lore from the Whitney Store

Top of Mount Whitney
AGE 14
July 1974
— Jacques
(Dad)

Whitney Portal Store, remodeled 1997

MOUNT WHITNEY:
Mountain Lore from the Whitney Store

A Collection of
Stories, Trail Tips, History, Recipes, and More
from the
Whitney Portal Store, est. 1935

Includes
COMPREHENSIVE TRAIL GUIDE

Doug Thompson
and
Elisabeth Newbold

Second Edition, Revised

Westwind Publishing Company, El Cajon, California

Cover design by Sam Newbold

Cover sketch by David Kirk

MOUNT WHITNEY:
Mountain Lore from the Whitney Store

A Collection of
Stories, Trail Tips, History, Recipes, and More
from the
Whitney Portal Store, est. 1935

by Doug Thompson
and Elisabeth Newbold

Published by:

Westwind Publishing Company
548 N. Westwind Drive
El Cajon, CA 92020

Copyright © 1997, 2003
by Elisabeth Newbold
First Printing 1997
Second Printing 2003, completely revised
PRINTED IN THE UNITED STATES OF AMERICA

Library of Congress Cataloging-in-Publication Data
Doug Thompson and Elisabeth Newbold
        Mount Whitney: Mountain Lore from the Whitney Store: A Collection of Stories, Trail Tips, History, Recipes, and More from the Whitney Portal Store, est. 1935 / by Doug Thompson and Elisabeth Newbold. - 2nd ed.
        p. cm.
        ISBN 0-9653596-1-1
        1. Mt. Whitney (Calif.)--Guidebooks. 2. Backpacking--California. 3. Hiking--California. 4. Sierra Nevada--Guidebooks. I. Title

Library of Congress Catalog Card Number: 97-60934

All photos are by the authors, unless otherwise noted.

Dedication

This book is another step in the passage along the Road of Life. It would not have been possible without all the people, places, and things we have experienced and stored up in our minds for some future time when the rivers run a little slower and grass is a little shorter.

The least important input into the making of the material was myself. The pieces of the picture come from the mountains, and from the time spent with so many people we have come to know. On trips into the many canyons and ridges, it is the exchange of humanness that happens when you share a hike or walk with someone who also understands that it is the flowers, trees, rocks and rivers, birds, bears, and the quietness of the desert that are the true success stories in our lifetime.

When we started to run the Store, we knew we would be tested on many fronts. We approached this adventure with the idea that we would try to adjust to the various demands as they arose. Even our wildest dreams could not come close to what we have experienced and learned since.

Nature has a very distinct cycle—we just don't know what it is. Once we accepted that bit of wisdom, knowing that today will only be like today once, we came to learn that in the morning new things will start and begin another today. Sometimes the experience will be snow, or sometimes bees, butterflies, ladybugs, ants or bears, waterfalls roaring or moon shining on the majestic walls that surround us. This is what we can dedicate a portion of this work to—our growing.

The most important people of my life are my family: my wife, son, brothers, mother, and their families; and my wife's family that came to this country from another, seeking all its hope and glory. What we have gained in our mountain experience has, at times, taken us apart from our family ties. I hope this will be recognized as a greater need, to be fulfilled with greater joy.

It would not be possible to close without a confession of my belief that we are passing through here as everyone else—no stronger, no braver, no wiser—just a little luckier that our stay will be a little longer.

To my wife, for the many nights she has been so tired that she couldn't sleep; and my son, who has grown into a man on this mountain, coming to understand his own self and nature. As a family, Mom, Pop, Son and Sonny, we hope we can flip a few more burgers, cook a few more hotcakes, take a few more walks, answer a few more questions, and help out on a few more rescues.

Thank you,
Doug Thompson

• • • • • • • • • • • • • • • • • • •

To my late Father, Eugene B. Barnes, Jr., in appreciation of his lifelong gifts to me: a love of walking in mountains among wild things, and a propensity for working with words.

To my husband, Max Newbold, in gratitude for his vision of this book, and his support in bringing it to fruition.

Elisabeth Newbold

Acknowledgments

The authors are grateful to the many people who helped in the writing and publication of this book. We gathered information and photographs from many sources, and appreciate all those who contributed to each edition, as follows:

- All visitors who signed the Guest Book for your "quotable quotes" sprinkled throughout
- George Marsh for material and photos on Gustave Marsh
- Sam Newbold for the cover design
- David Kirk for the cover sketch
- Tom LaRocca for his personal account of climbing Mt. Whitney
- Eric Jessen for research on the Whitney Portal cabins, and various photos
- County of Inyo, Eastern California Museum for historical photos
- Marc and Roger Moreau for photos of bears and more
- Sally Anderson for the photo of Doug Sr. & Newbolds
- Kendall Bradford for the action shot of Doug Jr. skiing
- Rick Erickson for summit photo via Mountaineer's Route
- Dave Morrison for his prize-winning photo of the Portal waterfall
- Gilda Garcia and Mark Brunke for photos of their summit wedding
- Russell Simon for photos and computer support
- Marcyn Del Clements for lists of flowers and birds, plus photos and a poem
- Bob Bacon, Eric Jessen, Martin Sweeney, Chris Riesen, Richard Dinkla, Russell Simon, Bob Rockwell, Larry Thompson, and Tom Davidson for help with proofreading

(continued)

Acknowledgments *(continued)*

- Earlene and Doug Thompson, Jr. for their recipes, ideas, proofreading, patience, and tolerance of all the interruptions this book's writing caused in their lives
- Max Newbold for his many good ideas and never-ending faith in us
- Bob Rockwell for 94th summit photo, information on the one-day hike, and much more
- Shawn Trueman for help with the weather chapter
- Tom Davidson for his summit photo and survivor attitude
- Bill Gookin for information on Hydrolyte (formerly Gookinaid)
- Colleen Heublien for the three-generation summit photo
- Warren Axtell for photos of a marmot and more
- Wm Ross for his professional postcard photos
- Gene & Jeannine Hauet for bear damage photo
- Chet & Barbara Hardin for computer back-up help
- Jim Stewart for aerial photo map
- Matai Sessions for help with maps
- Rochelle Keene for Big-One-In-One-Day testimonial and summit photo

Table of Contents

Warning—Disclaimer

LOOKING OVER WHITNEY CREST TO
THE GREAT WESTERN DIVIDE & KAWEAH RIDGE

LONE PINE LAKE

OUTPOST CAMP

BIG HORN PARK

MIRROR LAKE

MT. WHITNEY TRAIL

CONSULTATION LAKE

TRAIL CAMP

TRAIL CREST

MT. MUIR

KEELER NEEDLE

MT. WHITNEY 14,494 FT.

MT. RUSSELL

PINNACLE RIDGE

MT. THOR

TO PORTAL

ICEBERG LAKE

UPPER BOY SCOUT LAKE

MOUNTAINEER'S ROUTE

LOWER BOY SCOUT LAKE

NORTH FORK LONE PINE CK.

MT. WHITNEY
USC & GS EL=14,494.164

FIRST ASCENT AUGUST 18, 1873, C. BEGOLE, J. LUCAS, A. JOHNSON

FIRST TRAIL WAS BUILT IN 1904 BY LOCAL RESIDENTS. THE HUT ON THE SUMMIT WAS BUILT BY LOCALS IN 1909 FOR SCIENTISTS. THE TRAIL WAS REBUILT/RE-ROUTED SEVERAL TIMES AND PACK ANIMALS WOULD TAKE PEOPLE TO THE SUMMIT. PACK ANIMALS ARE NO LONGER ALLOWED ON THE TRAIL AND THE FIRST PART OF THE TRAIL, WHICH WAS STEEP, WAS CHANGED TO THE PRESENT LOCATION.

TRAIL MILEAGE AND ELEVATIONS

	DISTANCE		ELEVATIONS	
	MILES	KM	FEET	METERS
WHITNEY PORTAL TRAIL HEAD	0	0	8,360	2,548
JOHN MUIR WILDERNESS SIGN	0.5	.8	8,500	2,591
LONE PINE LAKE	2.5	4.0	9,850	3,002
OUTPOST CAMP	3.5	5.6	10,365	3,159
MIRROR LAKE	4.0	6.4	10,640	3,243
TRAILSIDE MEADOW	5.0	8.1	11,395	3,473
TRAIL CAMP	6.0	9.6	12,000	3,658
TRAIL CREST	8.2	13.2	13,777	4,199
JOHN MUIR TRAIL	8.7	14.0	13,480	4,109
MOUNT MUIR	9.0	14.5	14,015	4,272
KEELER NEEDLE	10.2	16.4	14,000	4,267
MT. WHITNEY SUMMIT	10.7	17.22	14,494	4,417.83

WWW.WHITNEYPORTALSTORE.COM

Full moon sets over Whitney Needles as rising sun's rays illuminate surrounding peaks

I. INTRODUCTION

If you're about to climb the Whitney trail, whether it's for the first time or the hundredth, you naturally have questions about weather, trail conditions, and rest room status. If you've just come down from the mountain, you bring back answers to these questions and more. You also want to talk to some fellow human beings and share your experience with people who appreciate it. For this reason, the Whitney Store has become a place of lively conversation.

> *"A real pleasure talking with you"*
> *-7/23/88, Richmond, VA*

The Store is owned by Doug and Earlene Thompson, and their son, Doug Jr. All three are gracious hosts, good listeners, and great story-tellers. This makes the atmosphere one of friendly camaraderie.

Mt. Whitney stories are served up with breakfast, lunch, and dinner, if you want to listen. But most people would rather talk, and they do. The societal barriers we keep around us for protection in our everyday lives are lowered in this place. The Mountain reminds us of our insignificance, and our brotherhood. Visitors realize more clearly how dependent they are upon each other, and strangers become friends easily and quickly.

Several books have already been written about Mt. Whitney. This mountain's story is a tale full of geological terms, botanical descriptions, historical accounts, and environmental concerns. Personally, we think everyone who has ever climbed Mt. Whitney could write a book about his or her own experience. Each book would be unique because each one's time on the mountain is a reflection of who this person really is.

This is not just another book about Mt. Whitney. It is also a book about you—people who are drawn to The Mountain for one reason or another. People come here from all parts of the world. Each one carries a unique set of expectations, led here by his or her own particular motivation. Almost everyone visits the Whitney Portal Store, a little country kitchen affair offering hot food, hot showers, hiking supplies, and souvenir T-shirts. The friendly folks who run the store have seen and heard it all—dumb questions, outlandish outfits, family arguments, life-threatening situations, life-changing events, and heart-warming heroics.

> 'Thanks for the info"
> -6/4/88, Surry, England

The humor, pathos, and drama of being human is evident in the microcosm of the Whitney Store. Visitors have left their impressions in the Guest Book and in the minds of the storekeepers. These tales are passed across the counter, free of charge, by the Thompsons. The Whitney Store offers more than money can buy.

This book is a collection of information related to Mt. Whitney and the surrounding area. In response to the huge volume of questions asked about the Whitney Trail, the "Store People" made up a few handouts with vital information about the area. These pages were the seeds that grew into this book, where you will find valuable details about climbing—insights gained through years spent at the Whitney Store—and a brief history of the area.

We have also included recipes for popular menu items served at the Store over the years. All this is intermingled with selected quotes from the Guest Book, previously unpublished photos, and stories of peoples' unique and interesting experiences. If you've been here before, perhaps you'll recognize your Guest Book entry or your own special story.

Many volumes of information were consulted during the research for this book.

> *"Doug gave great advice and makes a mean cheeseburger & fries"*
> *-9/2/00. San Pedro, CA*

One of the more difficult tasks in putting it together was not so much deciding what to include, but what to omit. We want to emphasize that this book is not intended to be a conclusive work. Its purpose is to offer a unique perspective of Mt. Whitney. It springs from a desire to share our experiences, and to help others discover their own.

Meeting our many visitors from around the world has convinced us that we all share a common need to return to nature. The Mt. Whitney area attracts people from all walks of life. Some bring a desire to conquer the mountain; some come just to experience it. Individual fulfillment can be found either way. Those who approach the mountain as an obstruction to be defeated are usually turned back by natural forces or their inability to adjust to them. We cannot control nature. Success comes by embracing it and letting our bodies adapt to it.

We have included a selection entitled "This Year or Never" in Appendix A describing one hiker's Mt. Whitney climb. This piece offers a fairly typical experience of one individual who set a personal goal and was able to reach it. The account is representative of how men and women respond as they pass through this area on their "Road of Life."

Some hikers come here with a lifetime of mountaineering experience, and some with absolutely none. Hopefully, this trail can be an introduction to how people can, by their own acts, enrich or destroy their own lives as well as the fragile environment. We are certain it is only the people who come to this mountain, and the choices they make, that control the impact on its ecology. It is not so much a factor of the number of people who visit Mt. Whitney, but of what those people do when they get here.

We hope you enjoy this book. Please stop by the Store and let us know how you liked it.

Whitney Portal Store
Operated under Permit from Inyo National Forest Service

P.O. Box 61
Lone Pine, CA 93545

In Season: 760-937-2257
Off Season: 909-734-7726

The Thompsons: Doug Sr., Earlene, and Doug Jr.

Doug Thompson Jr. says, "Thanks—without your support this wouldn't be possible." (photo by Kendall Bradford)

5

• •

Introduction to Second Edition

The time has come to print the second edition of the Mount Whitney Guidebook. We welcome the opportunity for correcting and editing names, and updating information. We've added new photos and quotes. Also, the reality that the reservation system will never stay the same has directed us to write that section with a new perspective. Included here are some thoughts and observations we've made over the past five years since the first edition was published.

> *"Thanks, Doug & Staff for your hospitality—Inyo CCC Trail Crew 2000"*
> *-9/9/00, Klamath, CA*

We now realize there is a critical lack of information on campgrounds. Data is available, but the challenge is finding it for all the campsites— federal, state, county, and private. It is also vital to know which places are available for advance reservation and which are open on a walk-in basis the day you arrive. (See FAQ #13, p. 18.)

Major improvements were made on the Whitney Trail during the 1998, 1999, and 2000 seasons. Large sections were reworked to repair snow and ice damage above Trail Camp, and erosion control and tread damage all the way down to the trailhead. A great job was done by the trail crews. A great deal of effort is needed to maintain the section from Trail Crest to the summit. With winter conditions for ten months a year, snow and ice damage requires almost constant trail repair and clearing. The last 400 feet of elevation gain and half mile of trail can be impossible to follow due to the many false trails and the snow that stands in the saddle around Keeler Needle.

Bears, Bears, Bears! Food, Food, Food! Cars, Trucks, Vans! Incidents of bears breaking into vehicles have increased to the point where new restrictions are now in effect in the Whitney area. You MUST use a bear canister while on the Whitney Trail. Do NOT leave food in your car while at the Portal—store it in a bear locker. We've added a new chapter devoted entirely to the bears.

We'd like to remind you to take your keys when you leave your car parked at the Portal, and give a spare key to someone in your group. We see people who purposely lock their keys in the car so they won't have to carry them on the trail. They expect to call AAA to get help. This is the wilderness, and you left those conveniences behind when you left the city. It's our observation that 99% of all calls from The

"Your website was helpful for doing Whitney"
-7/3/00, Brea, CA

Store to a locksmith are made by males. And, these guys aren't very patient when it takes a day or so to get a new key made and shipped up from the dealer in L.A. The airbags, front and side, tend to discourage locksmiths. Remember that special security system you bought? Now you are the thief, trying to break into your vehicle.

Our website, www.whitneyportalstore.com, has a message board where you should be able to review the postings and glean a wide view of the "Whitney experience." Visitors range from first-time hikers to someone who has hiked the Whitney trail for over 50 years, with close to 100 summits to pull from. Look at the photos, read the trip reports, enjoy the stories of bears and marmots, study the trail conditions, and the reasons why they summited or didn't.

7

We cover the trail in one separate chapter, and the day hike in another. Your success in reaching the summit is largely determined by the first step you take the day you start planning your trip. You are building the foundation of your journey. Stair steppers, tread mills, and gyms are good, and can condition you somewhat, but you need to build your long term endurance.

How? Stay on your feet actively for 10-12 hours. Experience the outdoors—wind, sun, rain and snow, and uneven ground. Sense how you process food and water, what body parts rub together, what small efforts you can take to reduce potential discomfort, and how you react to these discomforts.

> *"Doug - good book, thanks for advice"*
> *-7/10/99, Riverside, CA*

Every time it rains/snows or blows, the store fills with people worried about the weather. We came up with a universal weather report: "If you have to ask, you are probably not ready to go." I walked up to the Portal one winter's day in deep snow and high wind. I checked the store for damage and noticed a tent by the old trail head. I thought maybe someone was in trouble and went to check. I found a young man sitting on a rock drinking tea and eating raisins. We talked for hours, sharing tea and snacks. I walked home that night in the dark. We both understood the weather—he a doctor from Russia, and myself a kid from Kansas and Colorado. We had many stories to share about cold, and growing up playing outdoors in frozen clothes—the tingling and itching at night by the stove. Your concept of beauty is based on your file cabinet.

-Doug Thompson, April 2002

II. CLIMBING THE MOUNTAIN

As a species, we are programmed to continually seek for something higher and better. Mt. Whitney symbolizes "The Top" of the world as we know it, and gives us an uncomplicated task that can be completed in a relatively short time with a fairly large payoff: "I did it! I climbed Mt. Whitney!"

People climb Mt. Whitney for many different reasons. Some have done it to win a bet. Many seek to accomplish a goal they have set or to prove themselves. Others do it regularly as a pilgrimage for spiritual renewal. It serves as an escape from the complexities of our mixed-up world and gets us back to the basics—left foot, right foot, breathe in, breathe out. Physical exertion relieves our mental and emotional stress, and there is a great view to reward us for persevering!

> *"I did it! Yeeeehaw!!"*
> *-9/8/93, Valencia, CA*

One of the attractions of Mt. Whitney is that it can be enjoyed at all levels. There are trails and hikes to fit every person's skills and abilities. A toddler or someone in a wheelchair can enjoy the area around Whitney Pond. A beautiful, lush trail follows the south side of Lone Pine Creek from the Pond down to the Whitney Portal Campground. This leisurely one-mile hike can quickly relax your nerves and provide a peaceful escape. The Whitney Trail is a strenuous route to the summit; but the first two and one-half miles up to Lone Pine

9

Lake offer a good training ground for beginning hikers and include gorgeous views of Owens Valley. Another delightful variation is hiking the Trail by moonlight. Plan your trip around the full moon; you will find its light more than adequate, and will escape the heat of the day as well as the crowds. You will need a flashlight only in tree-shaded areas.

The Mountaineer's Route offers a good hike for "well-seasoned limbs," according to John Muir; and conquering the East Face, using ropes and special equipment, provides the rush that thrill-seeking

> *"Moonlight Ascent II"*
> *-7/21/89, Woodland Hills, CA*

climbers enjoy. For a description of the East Face climbs see Peter Croft's book, <u>The Good, The Great, and the Awesome</u>. Another challenge some have taken is a hike and/or bike ride from the lowest point in the continental U.S. (Badwater, in Death Valley, 282' below sea level) to the highest (Mt. Whitney)—both lie within Inyo County. You may choose to spend your whole summer in the mountains, following your dreams along the John Muir or Pacific Crest Trails, with Mt. Whitney being just a "tourist spot" along the way.

You are free to customize your visit to suit your needs and your schedule. We hope the information offered here will make it easier for you to plan and carry out your own Whitney Experience.

The Whitney Trail is one of the best-kept routes in the Sierra. Originally built in 1904 through efforts of the local townsfolk in Lone Pine, it has been rebuilt and rerouted several times.

> *"My legs & lungs are loving life!"*
> *-6/3/88, Pasadena, CA*

Today it is the most heavily-traveled trail in the Sierras. This may give hikers the impression it is an easy trail, and for some it is. Do not forget, however, that it is rated "very strenuous," and people have lost their lives trying to hike it.

Due to the length and the altitude, it is an arduous one-day hike. Most people do better if they split it up, planning at least one overnight stay along the way. This section contains information about the Trail, including a Guide pointing out landmarks along the way, common questions/answers, and special advice for those attempting to make the trip in one day.

Procedures for obtaining day and overnight hiking permits are subject to change. For current information, and to obtain the necessary permits, contact
Inyo National Forest
873 N. Main Street
Bishop, CA 93514
Phone: (760) 873-2483, FAX: (760) 873-2484
You can also try this website:
http://www.r5.fs.fed.us/inyo/vvc/permits.htm

> *"Breathtaking, from the top and the bottom."*
> *-10/9/00, Ramona, CA*

View of Mt. Whitney from Portal Road

•••••••••••••••••••••••••••

A. CLIMBING FAQs

This section contains a compilation of our best answers to Questions Most Often Asked at the Whitney Store. We hope this list of Q&As helps. We have heard them more times than we can count. Most of the answers come from people like yourselves returning from a hike and telling us what they experienced.

1. How far is it to the top?
Most sources say it is 11 miles from the Portal to the summit. A more realistic way to look at this trail is to

> *"It's a long way"*
> *-7/31/89, London, England*

think of it as **22 miles round trip**.

2. How long will it take ME to do it?
Use as a guide: one hour per thousand feet elevation gain, plus two miles per hour distance. Six thousand feet elevation gain (6,000/1,000) = 6.0 hours, plus eleven miles distance (11/2) = 5.5 hours, suggesting a total of 11.5 or **12 hours for a one-way trip up**. This trail is rated strenuous. Above Consultation Lake, sun and altitude can be a problem. (See "How Long Will It Take" on p. 101)

3. Can we see Mt. Whitney from here?
No. The mountain behind the Store is Thor Peak. The mountain to the south is Candlelight. If you travel back down

the road to the first sharp turn (1/2 mile) you will see Mt. Whitney on the right and the Needles just to the left. If you look at a postcard from the Store, you'll see how it looks from this location.

4. Can we make it in a day?

Some can, some can't. You have to decide for yourself. Remember, distance isn't the problem for a good hiker. It is the altitude that seems to knock most people back. Also, the faster you travel, the less time your body has to adjust to the altitude. (See next chapter, "The Big One In One Day")

> *"Oh, you mean this mountain"*
> *-8/25/93, Palo Alto, CA*

5. How hot or cold is it on top?

General rule: four degrees for every 1,000 feet up. Six thousand feet elevation gain (6,000/1,000) = 6 x 4 = **24 degrees difference between the Portal and the top**. So, if it's 60 degrees at the Portal, it's approximately 36 degrees on top.

Storms can come in very quickly. We have dropped 43 degrees in two hours at the Portal and have had snow in what was "shirt sleeve" weather. Wind can come up very fast and strong. On the back side (west) it can really add to fatigue and bring on hypothermia. Remember, at 40 degrees you are loosing body heat faster than you can recover it if you're not protected from the elements.

> *"Watch for hail at the Crest!"*
> *-8/9/89, Berkeley, CA*

Afternoon thunder storms are rare most of the year, but are not uncommon in July and August. You need to be ready for one at all times. Be prepared mentally to turn back if you face a storm. Lightning has been a problem on the mountain, especially when you are exposed on the ridges and above timberline. It has killed others and it can kill you.

6. Is the water safe to drink?

Maybe. Most water in the high country is safe. But some may not be, and some may vary based on the season. If you don't want to take a chance, boil, filter, or treat all your water before use. Please don't "doo-doo" or pee in the water. It sounds stupid, but why do you think some water is bad now?

7. What should we take for an overnight trip?

If you are in a group, share—don't take five of everything. Take warm clothing, windbreakers, gloves, hats, and extra socks. Don't forget the sunscreen and sunglasses. Take at least one flashlight, good sleeping bags, ground pad, and ground cloth (plastic). Go as light as you can, but be prepared

> *"Take something warm to the top! Be careful!"*
> *-6/14/88, Eugene, OR*

for a rapid change in the weather. Trim your toenails before you go. Wear shoes or boots that are well "broken in." Lighter boots, cowboy boots, or even sturdy tennis shoes are OK. The trail is very rocky and may bruise unprotected feet. Bring moleskin. Watch for early signs of blisters and treat instantly. We see people with feet that would sell tickets at a carnival.

8. Do we need a permit?

Yes. Anyone in the Whitney Zone must now have a permit for both day and overnight hikes. Call the **Inyo National Forest** at 760-873-2483 for information. FAX is 760-883-2484. Information is also available at the Mt. Whitney Ranger Station (in Lone Pine) at 760-876-6200, or you can visit them to request information or a permit. **Permits are not**

available at the Trailhead or the Store! See Forest Service flyers for more details, or try this website:

http://www.r5.fs.fed.us/inyo/vvc/permits.htm

9. Does anyone check for permits?

Yes. Rangers will turn you around if you do not have a permit, and they may impose a fine for each member of the group. Rangers are on the trail for your protection and enjoyment. Please follow all the rules and requirements in effect. The trail is used very heavily and it takes very little to destroy the fragile alpine environment forever.

> *"The Park Rangers deserve a raise"*
> *-7/21/89, Santa Cruz, CA*

10. What is the best way to get to the top?

We can't stress this enough: **It's a big mountain**, a **long distance**. Weather factors, altitude, and your own mental and physical makeup are all factors you must consider. Arrive at the Portal a day or two before you start the hike, if possible. Rest. Get your pack ready. Try a short shakedown walk. Get to bed early. Get up early. Do the first 2 miles before the sun gets too high—the first part of the trail is open and can get quite warm. Walk at a pace so the slowest/ weakest member of your party doesn't have to breathe hard. Also, don't hike so fast that you need to stop and rest, but do take a few minutes to rest about every hour.

> *"Rize n Shine - It's summit time"*
> *-7/18/00, Sacramento, CA*

Stop at Lone Pine Lake. Rest/sleep several hours. Continue to Trail Camp—no hurry, pace yourself. Set up camp, organize your day pack for the ascent, and get to sleep early. Get up early and travel as light as possible. Take clothing/wind-breaker, sunglasses, sunscreen, water, snacks, and basic first aid supplies. Hike to the summit. Always try to stomach breathe (yoga breathing) on the way up, for the air is thin and we tend to not get

> *"One-day climb was great. The website helped a lot!"*
> *-8/4/99, Simi Valley, CA*

enough air anyway. Enjoy the view and take a few moments to let what's around you happen. You have joined the silent family of people who have been on the mountain. Climbers often come up the various back routes, so please don't throw anything off the top. Hike back down to Trail Camp. Most people continue on down to the Portal the same day. If you have time, you may choose to sleep at Trail Camp again or hike down to Outpost Camp for your final night on the Whitney Trail.

11. Do people steal packs/supplies left at Trail Camp?

Yes, but at times you can find people staying there who will watch your packs. The biggest thieves are the fat, furry marmots. Secure all food in your bear can, unless preparing or eating, to prevent raids by these cute but hungry snackers.

12. How is parking at the Portal?

Parking is always a problem on the weekends. The overflow lot was completed in 1990. This lot is about 500 ft. below the Portal area with direct access to the backpacker campground. Please do not park overnight in the lot by the pond. This is for day use only, and the camp hosts will ask you to leave.

If you travel in a group on the trail, and you or someone else decides to turn back, don't assume everyone will meet at

the [any landmark in the area]. This causes a lot of problems.
Many calls to Search and Rescue (SAR) could be avoided if
people communicated about where they plan to meet. Please have a bailout plan so you can find each other.

> *"Nice to see a place which is not totally paved over"*
> *-8/2/90, Cupertino, CA*

This will help prevent SAR volunteers from wasting their time
and energy searching for you on the mountain when you are
actually sleeping in your car.

13. Where can we camp, at or near the Portal?

You can camp for one night only at the backpacker
campground which has eighteen walk-in sites (no reservation
needed). Also, Whitney Portal family campground is about one
mile down the road. They have 24 reservable sites, plus 18
non-reservable sites which are available on a first come first
served basis. If they're full, try Lone Pine campground (43
sites), five miles down towards town. There are several other
public, non-Forest Service campgrounds nearby: 1) Tuttle
Creek (BLM), 85 sites, no potable water; 2) Portagee Joe
(Inyo County), 15 sites; 3) Diaz Lake (Inyo County), 200 sites.

14. When is the best time to hike to the top?

Some years, snow or ice stays on the switchbacks and Trail
Crest until late June and nights are cool. July and August are
crowded. The first week of September can be hot. The crowd clears out

> *"What a view at the top room"*
> *-8/9/88, San Luis Obispo, CA*

about the third week of September. From this time to the last
of October is good, but be ready for an early snow or rapid
weather change, and don't rely on people on the trail for

assistance. **During the week is better than on weekends.**
About the last of August, snowstorms start moving through and
can cover the higher part of the trail. If the trail is covered with
snow and ice, you are no longer just "hiking," and you should
turn back if you are not prepared for the severest form of winter
mountaineering.

15. What books or maps do we need?

This book
probably covers
everything you need
to know. Check our
website and message
board, and talk with
Rangers and/or hikers

> *"Thanks for the great website
> & book - they helped me reach
> the summit!"*
> *-7/6/99, San Jose, CA*

coming down for up-to-the-minute trail and weather conditions.
Be sure to read the Forest Service handouts for current year
information on trail conditions and bears. You can get to the top
of Mount Whitney without a map. A rough sketch of the route
is included in the front of this book. If you want more detail, we
carry excellent maps at the Store.

16. Do most people get sick?

Nearly everyone is affected by the altitude on this
hike. Your symptoms may range from a mild headache to
severe nausea, disorientation, or worse. Someone in your party
should read about and understand altitude sickness. *Going
Higher (The Story of Man and Altitude)* by Charles S.
Houston, M.D. published by Little, Brown and Company is
well worth having, not only for the information by the author, but
also the 40 pages of bibliography.

17. Are there bears?

Yes. During the 1988 season, bears started showing up for supper at the Store. They can and will rip open your car while you're on the mountain. They recognize most food items by sight and smell. Most people underestimate

> "Great bear cannister deal!"
> -6/25/99, Seal Beach, CA

their strength and ability to search and destroy. Bears are pretty routine at Outpost Camp, and were sighted at Trail Camp beginning in 2000 . During the season, Forest Service Rangers check regularly to make sure all campers store their food in bear-proof containers—this is now a requirement, and you can be fined for not abiding by it. You **must** store food properly to keep it away from the animals. While your car is at the Portal, keep all food in the metal bear boxes provided. If a bear breaks into your vehicle, you may be cited, and your car towed off the mountain.

18. What services are available at the Store?

We sell milk, cold drinks, ice and beer. We try to keep last-minute hiking and fishing supplies on hand: water purifying equipment, socks, sunscreen, walking sticks, bear cannisters, bait, tackle, energy drinks, snacks, and film. We also

> "It is good having a store at this place!"
> -8/3/90, Kertogenbosch, Netherlands

offer souvenir items developed by the Store or for the Store: T-shirts, mugs, patches, hats, spoons, post cards, cedar boxes, and much more. We maintain a bulletin board and will try to pass information up the trail by word of mouth. Also, we try to keep a

Shopping for dinner at the Portal (photos by Marc Moreau)

daily report of the trail and weather by people like you stopping in and giving us updates.

19.   Do I have to drive all the way to Whitney Portal to get one of your T-shirts?

We've opened a second store right on Route 395 in Lone Pine: "Whitney Portal Store Too," telephone: 760-876-0030. Also, you can order items all year round through our website at: http://www.whitneyportalstore.com

---

"Great little store & Mtn."
-7/2/93, Smithfield, UT

B. THE BIG ONE IN ONE DAY

People constantly ask us for advice when planning or attempting to hike to the summit of Mt. Whitney and back in one day. Information in this chapter will help you accomplish the one-day climb. However, most of these suggestions apply to overnight hikers as well.

There are benefits and drawbacks to doing the whole hike in one day. Of course the greatest benefit is that you don't have to haul overnight gear up the trail. It gives you a great sense of satisfaction to "do it" in one day. It also saves time if you are on a tight schedule. On the other hand, it is a demanding hike-

> *"Whitney in one day brutal but beautiful"*
> *-8/11/93, Santa Rosa, CA*

people should know what they are getting into before attempting it. And, as with any hurried encounter with the wilderness, you will miss out on some of the subtle beauties and the deeper connection that sleeping on the mountain can bring.

What you Are Facing:

People who want to successfully climb Mount Whitney in a day have three formidable adversaries to overcome: 1) high elevation, 2) dehydration, and 3) exhaustion. Each can be a challenge, but there is much you can do to overcome them. Also, 4) hypothermia, can confront you at night, during storms, or at colder times of the year.

23

1) High elevation

- On the summit of Mount Whitney, the amount of oxygen is 20% less than that at sea level.
- High Altitude Illness (HAI) happens when your body doesn't get enough oxygen into the bloodstream. Symptoms are headache, weakness, fatigue, loss of reasoning ability, upset stomach, vomiting, and incoherence.
- HAI can appear as low as 6,000' and includes three conditions (see Going Higher, Dr. Houston for detailed information):
  - Acute Mountain Sickness (AMS)
  - High Altitude Pulmonary Edema (HAPE - fluid accumulation in lungs)
  - High Altitude Cerebral Edema (HACE- fluid accumulation in brain)
- Risk factors for HAI include:
  - Prior history of HAI
  - Living below 3,000' altitude
  - Exertion
  - Preexisting cardiopulmonary conditions
- Physical fitness is not protective against HAI
- Before the climb:
  - Acclimatize before climbing; this is the most effective, but it may take months for the body to adjust.
  - Ask your doctor about these prescription meds:
    - Diamox (acetazolamide)
    - Decadron (dexamethasone)
- During the climb:
  - Some people use ibuprofin or aspirin.
  - Doug avoids using antihistimes to treat congestion because of the negative effect on respiratory passages, and a dehydrating effect on the system

Numerous altitude studies have been done, and the body of knowledge continues to increase. For example, search the internet for the American Alpine Club.

Our personal preference is to adapt naturally, versus "tricking" the body with chemicals. We don't recommend using anything that would mask your body's natural warning system. If possible, sleep at

> *"Climbed in one Day!!"*
> *-7/16/92, Copenhagen, Denmark*

a higher elevation before your hike. The best method is to spend the day high, and sleep low, but if you live and work along the coast you can drive into the 5,000 - 8,000 ft. mountains and spend the nights.

We have seen hikers standing on the trail with eyes glazed, unable to speak clearly. These people should be taken down to lower altitudes without delay, but most will argue that they are OK and that they HAVE to make it to the top. The longer they stay, and the higher they go, the sicker they will get. This condition can be FATAL—get down to lower altitude IMMEDIATELY if you

> *"Don't try to climb Mt. Whitney in one day"*
> *-7/1/88, Monterey, CA*

or anyone in your group develops these symptoms.

2) Dehydration

- Hydrate as much as possible several days before your hike.
- Being at high altitude causes you to lose far more fluids than at lower elevations.

25

DEHYDRATION AND STRESS
(source: American Red Cross)

Fluid Loss (% Body Weight Loss)	Normal Temperatures	High Temperatures and/or Strenuous Exercise
1-2%	Impaired Judgement, Irritability, Headache, Muscular Aches	Sweating, Erythema (flushed face)
3%	Thirst reflex initiated, Lassitude, Sense of Fatigue, Loss of Appetite, Tight Sore Muscles	Profuse Sweating, Noticeably (to others) Impaired Judgement & Confusion*
4-6%	Profound Thirst, Dizziness, Muscle Cramps, Weakness, Fatigue	Very Irritable, may be Irrational, Pale, Severe Headache, especially at base of skull*
7-8%	Nausea, Vomiting, Severe Vertigo or Dizziness, somewhat Irrational, Severe Muscle Cramps, Staggering	Cold, Clammy Skin even though core temperature may be 104 degrees F or higher, May have Stopped Sweating*
9-10%	Collapse, Very Irrational, Unconscious	Pale Skin, Tense & Contracted Muscles, Pupils may be Dilated, Weak & Rapid Pulse, Low Blood Pressure, Shallow Respiration*

*Stages of **Heat Exhaustion**

DEHYDRATION AND STRESS
(continued)

Fluid Loss (% Body Weight Loss)	Normal Temperatures	High Temperatures and/or Strenuous Exercise
8-10+%	**Heat Stroke:**	Skin Red, Dry & Hot, Sweating has Stopped, Severe Headache, Extremely Weak, Numbness Tingling in Extremities, Muscles Tense & Convulsive, Confusion, Dark Urine (if any), Pupils Contracted, Pulse Strong & "pounding," Rapid, Shallow & Labored Respiration Delirious Unconscious Comatose

"Drink lots of H2O"
-8/9/90, Chula Vista, CA

- Dehydration compounded by low vapor pressure of oxygen results in changes in blood chemistry, making it more acidic and harder to absorb what oxygen is available.
- You won't feel like drinking; if you get dehydrated, you'll feel even less like drinking. Drink anyway.
- Snow is water; use a wide mouth container so you can add it if needed. However, add only in amounts that will melt; too much and you'll freeze the water in your bottle.
- Sucking on snow will give you some moisture but note that it also lowers your core body temperature.
- We recommend taking a liter and filtering water along the way to replace it. Strive for intake of at least a half-liter every hour, or one liter every 1,000 feet.
- Dehydration results in classic symptoms of heat exhaustion: muddled thinking, irritability, fatigue

Doug adds a package of Hydrolyte (formerly known as Gookinaid) to each quart of water. This electrolyte replacement drink has been found to reduce leg cramps and loss of overall energy. He also places a small pebble in his mouth to keep the moisture machine working. During the heat of the day, cut a lemon and suck the juice. This will clean your mouth so when you do drink you will taste the water and quench your thirst. At stream crossings, wet the back of your neck and hair to help cool down. Water is available up to 12,000 feet. From Trail Camp to the summit and back can be free of snow and runoff. Make sure you leave Trail Camp with enough water: one quart bare minimum.

> *"Nice hike, major headache at top"*
> *-6/15/89, Fairfield, CA*

More about Hydrolyte from Bill Gookin, who developed this high energy drink over 30 years ago:

"Shortly after Hydrolyte E.R.G. was developed we received a letter from a runner who spent his two-week summer vacations backpacking in the Sierras. Each year, after the first day, he would have a splitting headache and malaise, no appetite, feel lousy and often nauseous. He figured that it went with the high altitude experience. Then, he took some Hydrolyte with him, drank at least a quart every day, had none of the symptoms, and covered much more territory than ever before.

"Mountaineering expeditions report that Hydrolyte helps them keep going even above 20,000' with no muscle cramps or altitude sickness, and less fatigue even with 100-lb packs."

3) Exhaustion

- Climbing Mount Whitney in a day is *strenuous*—harder than running a marathon, according to some who have done both.

- Eat lots of carbohydrates and get lots of rest (no partying) in the days before your hike.
- Your body is a machine; don't run it on empty. Put fuel in the tank.
- Pace yourself. Don't go so fast you must stop and rest often. Do stop and rest for 5-10 minutes every hour. Drink and eat each time
- Hiking poles are invaluable. Use two.
- Try for one mile per hour going up (10-11 hrs total) and about 2 mph going down (5 hours) = 16 hour day.
- Go as light as possible (see below)
- Strive for nibbling all day while hiking, vs. stopping for larger meals
- Calories are most important. Don't worry about ratios of proteins/carbs/fats.
- When possible, eat carbos; these are utilized most quickly. However, any food that tastes good to you is better than things that are "healthy" but stay in your pack due to appetite loss.

> *"One ultimately grueling Day!"*
> *-9/3/90, Edwards AFB, CA*

- Bring and eat what YOU like = things you are more apt to tolerate at altitude. Examples: Jerky, candy bars (chocolate can get messy), lemon drops, Jellybeans, cheese, nuts. Take a treat or two for yourself.
- An instant cup of soup or tea can warm your body and your spirits (you'll need a small stove).

You are at the starting line of a marathon when you attempt Mt. Whitney in one day. However, unlike a marathon with gentle ups and downs, the trail is continuously up and continuously down, 10.7 miles up and 10.7 miles back. This puts an extended load on your muscles and other body parts, using them for a much longer period of time than you normally train. In order to condition your body accordingly, you would need to do the stair walker for about seven hours, then turn around and use a completely different system of muscles walking down an uneven trail with steps up to 18 inches high and a steep downward slope. Don't assume that because you worked out faithfully for 45 minutes daily that you will be in condition to hike to the summit in one day.

Never leave L.A. and drive to Whitney, sleep a couple of hours, jump up and take off up the trail. This is the most common formula for failure. Try to spend at least a full day at Whitney Portal. Get a good night's rest and start your hike about one hour earlier than you would normally get up. Waking up three hours before your body is expecting it will be hard.

If you leave the Portal around 5:00 a.m. you should be back by 10:00 p.m. The last 2.5 miles (Lone Pine Lake to Portal) are well lighted by reflections off the bright granite. You must be in this area by dark. From Trail Camp to Lone Pine Lake is very

> "Has anyone found that lung
> I lost on the trail?"
> -6/4/00, San Diego, CA

rocky, uneven, and not well marked-you don't want to hike it in the dark. You should leave the summit by 2:00 p.m. (July-Aug) to make Lone Pine Lake by dusk.

4) Hypothermia:

Hypothermia is a condition where the body loses more heat than it can generate to keep your internal organs warm. Lowering your core temperature causes loss of reasoning ability. It also causes severe shivering and loss of motion-you just want to stay put-and you may lapse into sleep. If your body temperature continues to drop, death can and will occur. This is why it is critical to travel with someone.

30

All members of your party must know the effects/ symptoms of hypothermia. Stay dry and never let anyone with hypothermic symptoms lie down and go to sleep. Once your body starts shaking, get warm! Add clothing, head gear, and upper body (chest area) direct body contact. Do not ignore these symptoms-drink hot liquids, do jumping jacks, and get down to a camp where you can stay warm!!!

> *"Make sure to wear sunscreen"*
> *-5/30/93, Los Angeles, CA*

What You Should Bring:

Everything listed can be discussed for hours-how/why take this, and not that. Here are some parameters:

- **Know that no one took you up the mountain and no one should be required to take you down.**
- Keep weight to an absolute minimum.
- Take enough to get yourself back down to the trailhead in the dark and in a snowstorm.
- Know your limits of physical and mental endurance.
- Get a day use permit.

What You Should Not Bring:

You do not need a map for this trip. You are going on the Whitney Trail, which is one of the better trails in the Sierra. It is like a road. If you have trouble following it, go back down-a map will not help you. A small, one-page trail description is your best guide for a one-day trip. Save room by sharing. For example, not everyone in your party needs to carry a first aid kit. (But do make sure that at least one person in your party is carrying first aid supplies.)

Going Light:

- Select gear and clothing with weight in mind.

- Go for a tuneup hike and pretend it's Whitney. When you get home, divide your pack into three piles: stuff you used all the time, stuff you used a little, stuff you didn't use. Get rid of piles #2 and #3 while staying safe (i.e., don't throw out your first aid kit just cause you didn't use it)
- If you can take 10 lbs out of your pack before you start, that is 10 lbs you don't have to carry up 6,200'. Ten pounds can mean the difference between making the top with a smile, and puking your guts out halfway up the switchbacks.

A one-day trip up Whitney isn't the time or place to test out a new piece of clothing or equipment. Everything you take and everything you do to prepare for this hike is critical. Most of the high dollar products, poly-whatever, etc., are hyped up by slick ad magazines. Do not bring any of these if you have not used and tested them yourself. Before you spend those hard-earned greenbacks, make the salesperson look you in the eye and tell you they would pay full price and risk their lives on it. You cannot buy security, you have to earn it yourself.

> *"Get good boots"*
> *-6/21/99, Los Angeles, CA*

Consider the items you already have in your closet before you rush off to go shopping. We see people who spend hundreds of dollars for special clothing, thinking it will help them. If the weather gets bad on your one-day hike, you need to turn around and come down the mountain whether you're wearing new stuff or not.

Here is what Doug wears: long pants, lightweight boots, T-shirt, long-sleeved button shirt (light color), and sunglasses. He brings a day pack—a fanny pack or book bag—containing the following:
- wool sweater, hat (bacalava), and gloves

- extra large trash bag (poncho or emergency sleeping bag)
- windbreaker
- Sunscreen (use especially on nose and top of ears). Above 11,000 feet you are exposed to sun without protection of trees. The sun burns right into you from reflection off snow and rock. The atmosphere is thin and second degree sunburn can happen fast.
- Hat with a brim (helps prevent sunburn on scalp and face)
- flashlight w/extra batteries/bulb
- very small propane stove with one pot/cup
- During June, Sept. or colder months, he adds a down vest or jacket, and long underwear

Ground Rules:

Never go alone! Go up together and come down all the way together. If your party separates, keep at least two in each subgroup. Set a pace that you can keep all day without stopping. Deep breathe. This takes practice but is a real help above 11,000 feet.

All of this is based on using your own common sense and your awareness of your own limitations. You should see a doctor and make sure you are in good health before starting this climb. Talk with your doctor about Diamox (a prescription that can alleviate altitude sickness) and any conditions you might have that could be affected by high altitude.

Many people have tried to set and break records (their own or others') for this one-day trip. Others just show up and take off, many coming into the Store afterward to reflect on their experience—how far they got, when they got sick, when the first blister showed up, when they realized how much slower you go at higher elevations, and how cold it got so fast. Remember: the important thing is not how long it took to get to the summit and back. It is the experience you had that day you took the walk that will stay with you all your life.

Rochelle Keene of Lone Pine relaxes on the Summit.
She recently joined the many who have climbed
The Big One in One Day

One More Big-One-In-One-Day Success Story

Rochelle:
This was my first attempt at climbing Mount Whitney. I'm 26 years old and have wanted to take this hike for 10 years. With the right knowledge, encouragement, and support, I made it in under 24 hours, going with seven friends.

I would like to encourage anyone with the desire, to make this hike a reality for themselves. If I can do it, I believe anyone can!

Doug:
Rochelle worked late the night before her hike. She got off at 11:00 p.m. and came up to the Portal. Our group took off shortly after midnight. We made several rest stops along the way, arriving at the summit around 11:00 a.m. As usual, going down was more taxing since everyone had been awake for so many hours. We all arrived at the Store before closing time.

Rochelle's successful experience is one more example of how the information in this book can increase your chances of attaining your goal to climb Mount Whitney. Whether you choose the one-day hike or an overnight trip, take the time to study and apply the advice herein.

Please be safe, and enjoy!

Mt. Whitney Trailhead: Your hike starts here

View from the Trail: First glimpse of Mt. Whitney!

C. TRAIL GUIDE

Climbing Mt. Whitney is like eating a Whitney Portal Store pancake—at first, the task seems overwhelming. However, you can break it up into manageable pieces. Take the trail one segment at a time, and always remember that the distance you are hiking up the trail must be doubled to allow for your return trip. Use this trail guide for day hike and overnight trips.

We've added some descriptive visualization as a tool to help you relax and prepare mentally as you study this guide.

Trailhead: Mile 0.0, 8,367 feet el. The Whitney Trail begins about 100 feet east of the

> *"It's not how far you go but what you learn along the way"*
> *-7/18/96, St. Thomas, USVI*

Store—look for steps leading up to the bulletin boards where the Forest Service posts information (you can too—messages for other hikers, lost & found, etc.) At first, the Trail leads away from the mountain. Don't let this confuse you—it soon makes a sharp turn back to the west and leads you through a series of switchbacks taking you up through a pleasant grove of pine trees. Chances are you will soon be peeling off outer layers of clothing due to the exertion of climbing and the warmth of the morning sun.

Visualization: Let's assume you spent several days at higher elevation (above 8,000') and are on your way up the

37

*Coming down Mt. Whitney Trail: Stream
crossing at North Fork of Lone Pine Creek*

trail (permit in hand). Let's start the visualization pro-
cess—seeing the granite walls, the waterfall, the trees and
the valley below, with the Inyo Mountains to the East. Feel
the cool morning air surrounding you and hear the busy
activity of the squirrels and birds as you walk, feeling
relaxed and full of energy, knowing the day will be pleasant
and enjoyable.

Carillon Drainage: Mile 0.5

Depending on the weather and the time of year, a little mud or a few inches of water cross the trail here. The growth thickens, giving more shade.

Visualization:
Take a deep breath
and enjoy the
feeling of stepping
into the wilderness
and away from whatever you do for a living.

> *"Thanks to the trail crew for a great trail"*
> *-7/22/88, Boulder, CO*

First Serious Stream Crossing: Mile 0.65

The North Fork of Lone Pine Creek gurgles across the trail here. Stepping stones offer a dry crossing. You can walk through the water too. Be careful! Beginning backpackers without boulder-hopping experience should be especially cautious. We have seen a lot of people who lose their footing here, resulting in a sprain or broken bone. Ice can make the rocks extra slippery on cold mornings. While it usually melts during the day, it may ice up again by late afternoon, causing a hazard for tired hikers hurrying down the last stretch.

Welcome to John Muir Wilderness

Visualization: The first stream crossing gives you a chance to either rock-hop or just walk through the flow. Hear the rush of the water and feel the mist in the air, creating a calm and peaceful respite.

Entrance to John Muir Wilderness: Mile 0.85, 8,480 feet el.
 The sign tells you where you are and what regulations you are expected to follow. **Before your trip**, contact the Inyo National Forest at 760-873-2483 for current information on permit requirements.

Visualization: Read the sign and start your journey up a series of switchbacks that will take you from the north side of the canyon to the south side. Look at the waterfall on

*the south side and follow this silver ribbon into the trees.
The trail goes across an open area where one can see the
effects of winter and wind. Look for tree tops that have
snapped in the wind, and observed how snow pushing on
the trees has forced them to grow with a permanent bend.*

The Trail offers many beautiful views of Owens Valley
to the east, as well as spectacular granite walls and peaks to the
north and south. By now you will realize that whether or not
you go to the summit, your trip has been worthwhile. You will
see hikers with all varieties and extremes of gear. Some folks
cover this part of the Trail in shorts, T-shirts, and sandals,
carrying nothing but a
bottle of water. Others
sport heavy boots,
snow suits, and 60-
pound packs with every

> *"Climb on, Dude!"*
> *-7/19/93, Flagstaff, AZ*

conceivable piece of climbing equipment dangling off their
backs. It all depends on how long you'll be in the wilderness,
and what you're planning to do there. At one point, Lone Pine
Creek provides a lovely gushing waterfall—most people cannot
resist the urge to snap a photo or two, but save some shots for
later.

*Visualization: Look up and to the right—there you will see
the rock work on the trail, and above it the slanting face of
Thor Peak. Turning to your left, Owens Valley opens into
full view. Look for the green ribbon on the far side of the
valley that is the Owens River bed. Notice the color on the
Inyo Mountains. As you cross to the south side of the
canyon, you will pass through a ¼ mile display of flowers
and ferns. Try to identify as many as you can. This area is*

Log bridge over Lone Pine Creek, just before Lone Pine Lake

Lone Pine Lake

over 9,000' in elevation and some of the plants will take a different size and shape.

As you approach Lone Pine Lake, the trail levels off. On your return hike down, this is where people coming up will inevitably ask, "How much farther is it to Lone Pine Lake?"

Visualization: You will come upon a series of logs that cross a small stream, just past a beautiful waterfall and a very large display of corn lilies. Look around the logs as you cross, and you should see trout swimming about. Continue up the trail through a nice stand of fir, where it takes you to the sandy area above Lone Pine Lake. This flat area allows you to stretch your legs out and prepare for the next section.

> "Lone Pine Lake on his own feet!"
> -age 3, 7/17/93, Lancaster, CA

Lone Pine Lake: Mile 2.8, 9,420 feet el.

A sign on a tree points to Lone Pine Lake, which lies at the end of a short trail forking left and down. You should take the time to enjoy this scenic spot—reward yourself for getting this far. Camping is allowed here (200 ft. away from the water), and if you're not in a hurry it's a good place to acclimate for a night. Mosquitoes are a problem at times. The lake offers beautiful reflections of the slope to the south, the trees, and the sky. Soak your feet in the cool water, or take the plunge and go for a refreshing swim. Refill your water bottle, and continue hydrating to replenish fluids.

Visualization: At the back of this draw the trail switchbacks to the right and into Outpost Camp. As you

43

walk this section, look to the east; enjoy the reflecting pool of Lone Pine Lake, and the valley beyond.

Big Horn Sheep Park: Mile 3.5

After a short climb past Lone Pine Lake, the trail soon levels out to a sandy area and then follows a ledge system up to the entrance of a large meadow: Big Horn Sheep Park. New maps show it as Bighorn Park; it has also been called Big Horn Flat or Ibex Flat. The trail crests at the east end of the meadow (a good photo spot for a view back down to Lone Pine Lake). A welcome downhill stretch leads into the Park. (This is the dreaded "Uphill" on the return trip.) At one time this area was a base for pack trains. The trail has been rerouted along

> *"It's a beautiful trail & lots of comaraderie!"*
> *-8/16/00, Redlands, CA*

the south side of the Flat due to "free-for-all" tramps across the meadow that nearly destroyed it in the 70's.

Visualization: As you enter Outpost Camp area, the trail drops into a meadow alive with flowers and activity. The trail follows the southerly side of the meadow. At the west end you will see a magnificent waterfall where the trail bears right into Outpost Camp.

Outpost Camp: Mile 3.8, 10,360 el.

Congratulations—you have passed the 10,000' elevation level! Outpost Camp is located at the west end of Big Horn Sheep Park. This area is ideal for camping due to its level spaciousness and lovely shade trees. Lone Pine Creek provides a large and beautiful waterfall (and plenty of drinking water) just to the south. There is a solar toilet; if it is closed, there is ample topsoil for burial of fecal waste (unlike Trail

44

Ann Axtell visits solar toilets at Outpost Camp
(photo courtesy of Russell Simon)

Camp). A day hike to the summit can be made from this spot, leaving behind the extra pounds of overnight gear. This camping area is always less crowded than Trail Camp, more esthetically pleasing, and offers much better protection from wind and cold.

Visualization: There is another water crossing here that again can be "hopped" via stones, or you can walk through it. A short distance ahead you will see a sign for the solar toilet, and the next section of short switchbacks.

Mirror Lake: 4.3 mi., 10,640 el.
　　The Trail climbs steeply up a series of switchbacks to Mirror Lake. While overnight camping is prohibited here, it is a pleasant rest stop. Fishing is a possibility as well as swimming (although the water is always cold). Another series of switchbacks climbs up to the south, providing photogenic views

View of Mirror Lake

Mt. Whitney Trail just above Mirror Lake

of Mirror Lake from above. At this point the trail becomes very rocky, and trees thin out as you approach timber line.

As the Trail curves west, more views of Owens Valley below invite you to use your camera—be sure you don't shoot up all your film! We know of more than one climber who has done so on this breathtaking route, leaving no exposures for the summit (big mistake!). Make sure you drink water as you continue to climb. It will help minimize effects of the altitude, and drainage along this part of the Trail offers many opportunities to refill your jugs. Say goodbye to trees as you pass the last few twisted specimens.

Visualization: Soon you will arrive at the east end of Mirror Lake. During peak runoff periods, the rock stairs are

> "Wish we had somewhere like this back home"
> -6/6/90, Stockport, England

covered with water and you will need to walk along the edge of the rock, heading for the sign: "Mirror Lake—No Camping." Now travel up and left to the next set of switchbacks. This leads you through the last stand of trees and on to the granite slabs that bring you to Trailside Meadow.

Trailside Meadow: 5.3 mi., 11,395 el.

Formerly known as Ram Horn Park, this colorful little area provides a welcome visual relief from bare rocks, granite, snow, and sky. Lone Pine Creek flows through it, watering the many wildflowers and shrubs. Marmots live here, and may entertain you with their whistles and "woofs." Rangers are often seen here too—make sure you can find your Wilderness Permit if they ask to see it. No overnight camping is allowed.

Consultation Lake, with Arc Pass above

Party at Trail Camp (1993) Standing (L-R): Max Newbold, Jake Aguiar, Steve Daynes, Elisabeth Newbold, Roger Moreau, Katherine Daynes. Front: David & Marc Moreau. (photo courtesy of Roger Moreau)

Visualization: Drink in the beauty above and below as you pass through this lovely spot. Listen to the cooling, rushing stream from Consultation Lake, and spend a few minutes looking at the fledgling flowers against the stark rock. Notice how great you feel, and be aware of how easy it has been drawing in energy and exhaling tension with every breath.

Consultation Lake: 5.8 mi.

This is the most misunderstood lake on the Whitney Trail. Some people call it "Constellation" Lake. Although this name is prettier, it is incorrect, as is "Consolation Lake." Consultation Lake is located to the left and above the Trail, about

> *'Superbe et Grandiose"*
> *-7/4/93, Paris, France*

a half mile before Trail Camp. Exhausted hikers who are concentrating on putting one foot in front of another, and on continuing to breathe, may miss it altogether. The unnamed ponds at Trail Camp are often mistaken for Consultation Lake.

For those who have the energy and inclination to explore, there are several campsites at and above this beautiful lake which are cleaner and less hectic than Trail Camp.

Visualization: The trail now moves on to another set of switchbacks that exits at Trail Camp. As you walk through this area, the ridgeline surrounds you and the giants start to appear before your eyes. You are now at 12,000' and the towering granite face is only a stone's throw away.

Trail Camp: 6.3 mi., 12,039 feet el.

This is the most popular camping spot on the Trail. While there are some good arguments for spending the night here, there are also many reasons for finding another place to sleep. Trail Camp is ideally located for two-day hikers because it puts them in the right place for a fresh start in the morning. The trouble is, so many people stay there that it has become polluted. During the busiest season, this camp is crowded, noisy, and it stinks! The solar toilet is off to the right; if you need to use the facility, please follow all the rules. Unfortunately, if the solar toilets are closed, campers use the area immediately surrounding them, and there is no soil to bury fecal waste. It sits out on the open rocks, decorated with wads of used toilet paper. PLEASE DO NOT FOLLOW THIS BAD EXAMPLE! There are alternatives, such as the kitty litter bag (see chapter on "Toilet Troubles").

> *"Biggest pile of rocks I've ever seen!"*
> *-9/14/89, Bakersfield, CA*
>
> *"Come to Colorado—there are all kinds of rock piles"*
> *-9/14/89, Denver, CO*

Another reason to avoid using Trail Camp as your base is the harsh weather conditions. Violent winds have destroyed tents or blown them away. The lack of topsoil means there is no dirt to anchor tent stakes. There may be snow on the ground until mid-July. By late August, storms can blow in suddenly, leaving a blanket of up to six inches of snow. It is a rocky, barren place—a little like camping on the moon (except for the water).

Unfortunately, some marmots have made a living off the leftovers at Trail Camp. Bear canisters are REQUIRED.

Don't share snacks with these cute little guys, either purposely or by accident—it's not the best thing for their health.

Mount Whitney Marmot
(photo courtesy of Warren Axtell)

At busy times, this Camp is also polluted with the sounds of radios, CD players, and loud voices. Be respectful of others and of the wilderness. Bright lights are also an unwelcome distraction. A small flashlight is essential (unless the moon is full), but bright lanterns are out of place.

Water sources at Trail Camp are the most likely to require purification treatment. You'll need to tank up for your climb to the summit. There is a possible water source about one-third up the

"Marmot stew tonight!"
-7/23/88, Santa Barbara, CA

switchbacks, depending on the time of year and the time of day.

Visualization: As you walk towards the west, you can see the trail going up the slope first to the south, then to the north, to catch Trail Crest.

Switchbacks: 6.5-8.5 mi., 12,039-13,777 feet elev.

Some people will tell you the switchbacks are easy, and others say it's the hardest part of the climb. One thing most everyone agrees on—they're boring! How many switchbacks are there? While that all depends on what exactly you count as a "switchback," the number is somewhere between 98 and 100.

51

CAUTION: Just because someone suggested you take an ice ax and crampons, these items are of little or no value—even harmful—if you don't have skill or experience in using them. This is why we don't stock these items at the Whitney Store for last-minute purchases. Even though we could make a lot of money selling them, we feel it would be criminal to lead people into a situation that could be deadly. Unless you already own the proper equipment, have used it, and know how to self-arrest, you are better off to turn back at this point. If the switchbacks are covered with snow, the trip is no longer a "hike"—it's full winter mountaineering.

This part of the trail is smooth and well-constructed, making it often possible to swing your legs, giving momentum for each successive step. Typically there is snowmelt running across the trail at regular intervals, and you should continue to drink lots of water. Don't think that just because it came from snow, it is pure. Always treat your water. Polemonium, a high-altitude, deep purple wildflower, spruces up the decor if you are climbing in July or August.

There are cable railings along a steep area of the Trail. While they were installed to provide help and safety along the way, use caution. Ice can be a problem on the switchbacks, and these railings sometimes give hikers a false sense of security. This is another spot where accidents happen due to early morning or late afternoon ice on the trail, or on the railings themselves.

Some years, snow covers the switchbacks as late as mid-July. It is impossible to follow this route until it has melted. The alternative is a chute just to the north of the switchbacks, which can be climbed in snow by experienced mountaineers.

Visualization: This section of switchbacks allows you to go into the coast mode—just moving along effortlessly, breathing deeply and exhaling with pressure. Looking along the trail for Sky Pilot and Sierra Golds, you are impressed with your own innate ability to prepare for this experience. You have hydrated with just the right amount of liquids. You have eaten just the proper kinds and amounts of food for the trip. Your shoes are the very best choice, and your clothing is keeping your body at the perfect temperature. With very little effort, you arrive at Trail Crest.

> *"Damn, this mt. is high!"*
> *-7/16/00, Pleasanton, CA*

.

Trail Crest: 8.5 mi., 13,777 feet el.

When you get to Trail Crest, you have reached the summit, for all intents and purposes. You can look over the ridge and feast your eyes on the vastness beyond—the headwaters of the Kern River, and many peaks and valleys of the Western Sierra. You have attained an altitude just short of that at The Top, and your efforts are well rewarded by the magnificent view. A sign marks the dividing line between Inyo National Forest and Sequoia National Park. You now enter the National Park system (leaving behind the National Forest Service), which is run by a different part of the U.S. Government, and patrolled by a different set of Rangers.

Cables: Some seasons this area holds snow and ice until mid July. Note the shadow—this spot faces north, so does not get direct sun for most of the year.

Marc Moreau at Trail Crest. Behind him and to the West are Hitchcock Lakes and the Kaweahs (photo by Roger Moreau)

Visualization: Now you have the 360-degree view of the world below at 13,777' elevation. Look to the west and see the grand vistas of lakes, meadows, and ridge lines. Turning south, you marvel at Discovery Pinnacles, Arc Pass, and the Cottonwood Lakes area. As you move along, the summit of Whitney appears. Your route will be downhill now for a little while, and the trail becomes rocky and more uneven. But, knowing how well you have done this far, you will move forward with ease, always taking the right step and feeling secure as you progress toward your goal.

John Muir Trail Junction: 9.0 miles, 13,480 feel el.

After reaching Trail Crest, you will come upon a welcome downhill stretch which takes you to a fork in the Trail. To the left is the route to Crabtree Meadows, down the "back side" of Whitney. To the right is the final approach to the summit. Either way you turn, you are now on the famous John Muir Trail.

Visualization: The summit and the hut are in view now. As you walk along the west side of the ridge, the trail becomes more rugged, with short ups and downs, a narrow pathway, and uneven steps.
Ahead you will pass the John Muir Trail fork that heads to Yosemite. Make a mental note of this site because as the hikers come up from the west (Guitar Lake, Crabtree Meadows), most will leave their packs around the signs or group in the area for a break.

John Muir Trail Junction (photo by Russell Simon)

55

NOTE: ON YOUR WAY BACK from the summit, be sure you turn left—uphill—to come over Trail Crest and retrace your steps down the Whitney Trail. REMEMBER as you come back from the summit, the return trail to HOME— Whitney Portal (on the east side of the mountain), your car, the road, all of these important things, are on the trail that heads UP to get down. Every year we have people who take the wrong direction, which sometimes leads to a rescue operation. Make a little song, "Sometimes I got to go up to get down."

A short distance down from the junction, there are some tent sites where adventurers may decide to camp. Waking up to a sunrise here is a very memorable experience, but plan ahead for a cold night and for your water needs. Be sure you are carrying enough; there is no reliable source along this section.

> *"How 'bout that altitude"*
> *-6/5/91, Indianapolis, IN*

The Trail along the west side of the ridge to the final peak is another "photo opportunity" for marvelous views in every direction. Between the Needles, you can look eastward down upon Lone Pine, and across Owens Valley to the Inyo Mountains beyond. With a turn of the head, you can see the Kaweahs towering on the other side, and the deep trench of Kern Canyon. Looking closer, you will easily identify Guitar Lake below (it is shaped like a guitar), and various peaks to the north and south.

Because of the high altitude, hiking the last two miles to the summit can be taxing, even though the trail is not steep. Your mental acuity may decrease due to lack of oxygen to the brain. Headaches are common, as well as nausea. Like morning sickness, this is best treated by eating a small snack. Drink water, even if you don't feel thirsty. If symptoms increase, be aware that you will not get better until you GO

Summit hut: Julio, Carlota, Martin, and Dave

BACK DOWN TO A LOWER ELEVATION. If you begin vomiting, your body is losing too much liquid. The only cure for altitude sickness is to GET DOWN.

We should mention the various landmarks along this final ascent. Mt. Muir, elevation 14,015, rises to the right a short distance from the fork in the Trail. A mile further, Day Needle and Keeler Needle can be seen to the right. There is one particularly exposed point along here where both sides of the Trail drop off steeply. Anyone who suffers from the fear of heights (acrophobia) should not attempt this trail.

As you near the summit, you will meet people coming down. Many of them will encourage you—just as others encouraged them. You are almost there!

Visualization: *Moving along now, the summit is only 1.9 miles from the John Muir Junction. The last little area of confusion is just below the summit. The trail may be hard*

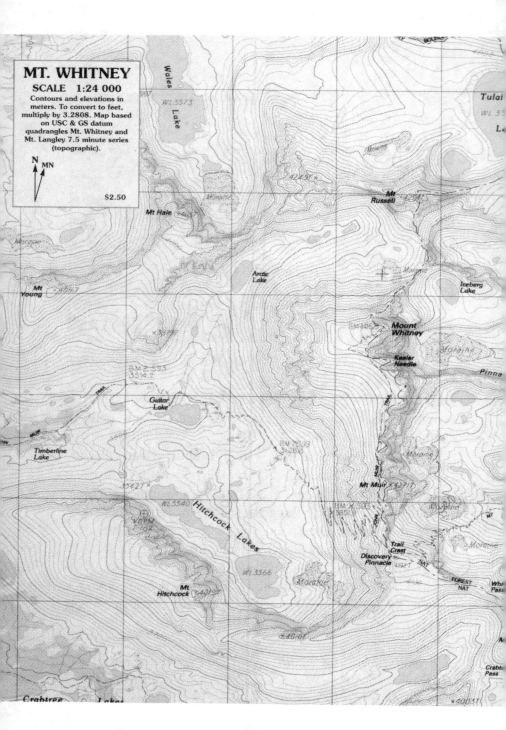

MT. WHITNEY

SCALE 1:24 000

Contours and elevations in
meters. To convert to feet,
multiply by 3.2808. Map based
on USC & GS datum
quadrangles Mt. Whitney and
Mt. Langley 7.5 minute series
(topographic).

N MN

$2.50

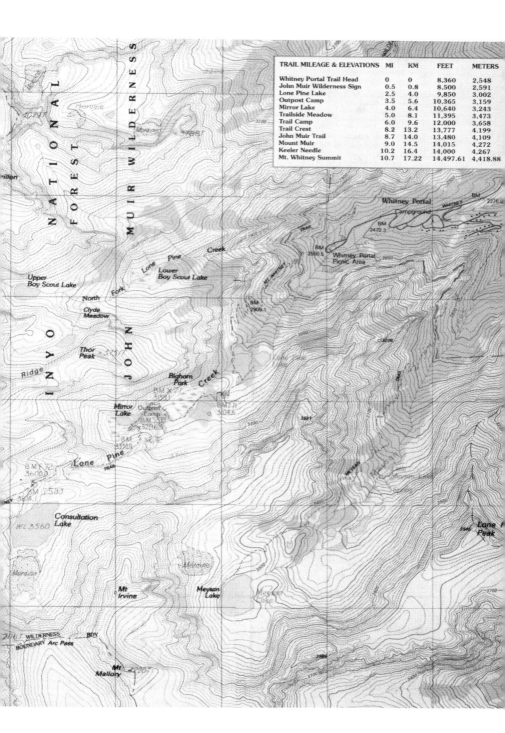

TRAIL MILEAGE & ELEVATIONS	MI	KM	FEET	METERS
Whitney Portal Trail Head	0	0	8,360	2,548
John Muir Wilderness Sign	0.5	0.8	8,500	2,591
Lone Pine Lake	2.5	4.0	9,850	3,002
Outpost Camp	3.5	5.6	10,365	3,159
Mirror Lake	4.0	6.4	10,640	3,243
Trailside Meadow	5.0	8.1	11,395	3,473
Trail Camp	6.0	9.6	12,000	3,658
Trail Crest	8.2	13.2	13,777	4,199
John Muir Trail	8.7	14.0	13,480	4,109
Mount Muir	9.0	14.5	14,015	4,272
Keeler Needle	10.2	16.4	14,000	4,267
Mt. Whitney Summit	10.7	17.22	14,497.61	4,418.88

Elisabeth and Max Newbold at the summit. You are facing North.

to follow due to false trails, snow patches, and rockslides covering it for short sections. Look left along the same contour you are standing on, and the trail is on this contour for several hundred feet. Then switchbacks lead up to the summit area. About ten minutes will take you through this area and then the hut is visible. No one can stop you now!

> *"Sleeping on Mt. Whitney was the greatest night of my life"*
> *-7/25/90, UK Forces, Germany*

Summit: 11 miles, 14,497.61 feet el.

What can we say about the summit that has not already been said? Sign the register; catch your breath; rest awhile; exchange a high five or two; eat your trail mix; take lots of

Russell Simon at the summit
(photo courtesy of Russell Simon)

photos; enjoy the jets if they fly by; try identifying all the surrounding peaks; and get out of there by 2 p.m. if you are
planning to go all the way down today. You still have a long
hike ahead of you, and you must reach Lone Pine Lake by
nightfall.

On the other hand, you may be planning to sleep at the
summit. This can be hazardous—storms are unpredictable and
lightning is a fatal force. However, if you are prepared, and the
weather is good, go for it—set up camp and get acquainted
with any others who have the same plan. We know of a group
of over 15 backpackers who camped on the summit to celebrate the 85th birthday of one in their party. It was his elev-
enth climb. They even had a birthday cake! His wife participated by hiring a plane and flying over the top.

Going Down

Lets go over the hardest part of the trip: "going down." All of the things most people do are focused on getting to the top. Well, that's exactly half way. At the top you will notice your feet have swollen, your socks are wet, your lips are chapped, and your bottom is covered with heat rash. Your feet have slammed into the end of your boots leaving your big toes very sore. Your shoulders are raw from an overloaded pack, and half the gear you bought is in some kind of disrepair or lost. Your eyes are red, and exposed skin like the tops of your ears, your nose, the back of your neck, and your legs are sunburned. You are tired and just want it to be over.

> *"I swear it is farther coming down than going up"*
> *-7/2/89, Shingle Springs, CA*

The trail takes on a different persona going down. You are now resisting motion downward and forward. As you move along the trail, the solid placement of footing and pressure loading is turned into quick front foot placement and pushing off with the other leg on smooth even sections. This is great, but from the summit to Outpost Camp that doesn't exist. What you have is uneven, rocky, slick, gravel-covered trail that is driving you forward. You now have to think about every step's placement: Is it solid, not tilting or slanting, and stable so that as you lift the other leg will the footing hold?

We cannot emphasize enough that reaching the summit is only half the battle. The hike down uses a whole different set of muscles, and holds its own potential for disaster. Folks coming down are usually fatigued, careless, and thus more susceptible to falls. They may not be disciplined about staying with their party. This can result in the problems of separation, miscommunication, misunderstanding, and an unnecessary call to the Sheriff's Search and Rescue Operations.

We see many people leave the summit and travel too far down the back side. Then when all the false trails run out, they see people along the trail and have to climb up to join it. As sunlight diminishes, it becomes more difficult to stay on the trail and avoid accidents. With the dark comes the cold, the risk of hypothermia, and the formation of ice on the wet areas of the trail.

Walking sticks and ski poles play a very big role in balance and allowing one to take the shock off feet, ankles, knees, and lower body by placing an extended pole in front of you and steadying yourself with it as you **gently** place your foot. Most people who use poles say that coming down without them would have been a lot worse. Some even tell us they couldn't have made it down without them.

> *"Thanks for the poles! Wouldn't have made it without them"*
> *-6/26/00, San Diego, CA*

Should you buy them? That's your decision, but you should never pass the chance to rent them or borrow them. We take them on every trip, and when one of us goes up to help someone down, we will not leave until we find an extra pair. These people who need help are generally exhausted, and usually have a problem with feet, ankles, or knees, and are moving slowly. Offering them the poles, and taking their packs, we can usually get them to walk to the Portal.

Stay together as you make your descent. This could save your life, or someone else's. Be aware of what is happening around you and be willing to give help where needed. You got yourself up the mountain and you are expected to get yourself down. If someone is in trouble, don't pass them by—find out what is wrong and make it right if you can.

Some people think they are doing someone in trouble a favor by hurrying past them to report the problem to the Store. This causes a longer delay in getting help than if the "message bearer" would have just given the needed help, sending someone else down with a report.

Another problem people have coming down is their loss of focus. They are thinking, "It's over, it's easy going downhill." Well, it's about the same amount of time coming down as going up. Look around and take in the view you may have missed on the way up. Talk with hikers going up. Do a little investigation on how they

> *"Very hard but glad that I made it"*
> *-6/25/89, Dallas, TX*

really look. What is their skin color, how are their eyes, speech, spirit level, pack size, shoes, and gear. File this away for your next experience. What we have learned is, "Everybody has the right stuff." By noticing what seems to work and what doesn't, you can save yourself some trial and error.

On the way down, look for short goals to reach. "When I get to ___, I will have a snack. I will look at the waterfall, take a picture of Mirror Lake from above, etc." Chances are you will only do this once, and your experience on film and/or stored in the big database you are equipped with should be loaded.

From Outpost Camp to the Portal, the trail is somewhat forgiving. It is mostly dirt and easy to follow. If evening sets in, you should be OK the rest of the way down. You can see the lights of Lone Pine show up, and watch the headlights of cars going up and down the Portal Road.

Having a flashlight will help. Watch the stream crossing at North Fork of Lone Pine Creek—it can be crossed by walking through the water. (We have gone to this area a number of times to help people cross in the dark.) After this crossing, the parking lot and campground appear. Now you have the chance to look up the canyon and see the hiker's flash-lights coming down. Many

> *"We climbed the Rock—and lived!"*
> *-6/5/88, Culver City, CA*

nights this will go on until early morning, and about 2:00-3:00 a.m. the early starters will head upward. Once we asked a group why they wanted to start so early. Their response was, they didn't want to walk in the dark.

Trailhead: 22 miles, 8,367 feet el.

Congratulations—you made it! Now you can cel-ebrate—treat yourself to whatever luxury you've been thinking about (hot shower, cold drink, fresh food, etc.). When you get home, please take the time to record and post your trip at www.whitneyportalstore.com. The Store's message board has become a busy place where you can share your experience and your photos.

> *"Made it to the top and thought about buying a hamburger the whole way down!"*
> *-8/3/00, Huntington Beach, CA*

Inyo County Sheriff's Dept. volunteer Search & Rescue Party on Mt. Whitney Trail: Andy Lehr, Jason Foster, Arnie Peterson

IMPORTANT - CELL PHONES

If you are relying on a cell phone for emergencies, it must have analog available and you should be able to reach the cell site in Lone Pine. If you dial 911 from a cell phone while on Mt. Whitney, it goes to the Highway Patrol in Barstow, California. You will get a quicker response by dialing Inyo County Search & Rescue/Sheriff's dispatch at **760-876-5606**. Carry this number with you; it can help expedite the rescue process and may even save a life.

• •

D. WHEN SOMETHING GOES WRONG

1. The Saturday Night Special

The Store owners use this expression—The Saturday Night Special—to describe a phenomenon that has become almost as predictable as Old Faithful during peak season. Business is winding down after a crowded, crazy day. We are tired, but we know it's Saturday night, and the fun isn't over yet.

Inevitably, someone comes in around 9:30 p.m. to report their friend or relative is lost on the Mountain. The person is beginning to panic because they suddenly realize the potential for disaster as night sets in. They may have been up and down parts of the trail several times searching for the missing person. Why does this happen? What can be done about it?

Traffic on the Whitney Trail peaks over the weekend. Hikers take off work early on Friday, drive up to the Portal, and head up the trail on Saturday morning. The majority of them have not taken the time to study and prepare for the trek. They envision a quick "mountain high" over the weekend, and do not think ahead, or discuss all the potential scenarios with their partners.

If a party consists of more than two people, they may not feel any need to stay together. The faster climbers might go ahead while the rest of the group sets a slower pace, planning to meet at the summit. Any number of things can happen to cause a missed connection. Slower hikers will not reach the summit in one day and may decide to turn back. Adventurous climbers may stray off the trail to capture a particular view on film or examine a cluster of wildflowers more closely. The net result is, the sun goes down without everyone knowing where everyone else is. Suddenly they want help.

What should you do if someone in your group is missing? Spread the word, and look for them in an organized fashion; if not successful, get help. When? The answer depends on a number of factors: age of the person (elderly, a child, or neither); their physical and mental condition; their clothing and gear; the weather, location, time of day; and more.

> *"[12:15 p.m.]...a hiker was heading down the trail. He was trying to get word through that someone was in trouble."*
> *-Tom LaRocca, "This Year or Never," 7/79*

Another common case of The Saturday Night Special occurs with a couple when one person has trouble getting down, and the other leaves to come down for help. The irony in this situation is that if you leave your friend in trouble on the mountain alone, you have just deprived him or her of the best help available—your own presence. Most people have more ability to help their friends overcome adversity than they realize. If your friend is developing hypothermia, give up your extra jacket. Put your arms around him or her. Do some jumping jacks together, and get their body temperature up.

If someone in your party is suffering from altitude sickness and dehydration, the worst thing you can do is leave that person on the trail. If someone is weak, take that person's pack for awhile and help them get to a lower altitude. Remember the song, "Lean on Me." If someone is feeling faint, offer some water and keep up the encouragement. Leaving someone alone on the mountain in a weakened condition is a life-threatening choice. THINK CAREFULLY before you do it. No one else can make the decision. YOU have to choose, based on the situation. If you must separate (i.e. broken bones, can't walk) make sure they have extra clothes, shelter, food, water, and if possible, some company. Most hikers are kindly people, and like to help if they can. The problem is that our society has numbed a lot of people's initiative so they don't realize they can help unless someone else makes the suggestion. Use your imagination. Use your sense of self-reliance. Take charge and show you care—it may save a life.

When we are faced with The Saturday Night Special, we have the unpleasant job of telling the distraught hiker some bad news. First, rescue efforts made during the night are on

> *"Worth every step! Go with a good friend"*
> *-7/15/90, Santa Barbara, CA*

foot only, since landing a helicopter on the Mountain after sundown is impossible. Second, the Sheriff's Department must evaluate the situation first and determine whether or not to call out the Volunteer Search Party. Third, a few pointed questions often bring the person to the unpleasant realization that they could have, and should have, taken care of the problem themselves.

2. Rescues

It must be made clear that THERE ARE NO RESCUE CAPABILITIES AT THE PORTAL. Many visitors to this area do not understand the concept of "Wilderness." This has led to many troublesome confrontations with distraught party members about the lack of instantaneous resolution to emergency needs.

Many people have misconceptions about the process of initiating, organizing, and conducting a rescue. A number of different agencies and organizations are available to perform rescue operations, but there are limitations on what can be done, depending on the time of day and the seriousness of an incident.

When an injury is reported, the Sheriff's Department is contacted and given all information available. If they determine that an injury is minor, and night has fallen, the most likely course of action is to notify a volunteer search organization to mobilize for an early morning start if the party does not come down under his/her own power.

> *"[4:15] ...we saw a rescue helicopter overhead...it was definitely searching for someone in distress....We were about three quarters of the way down the switchbacks when we saw the helicopter on the ground at Trail Camp."*
> *-Tom LaRocca, "This Year or Never," 7/79*

If an injury is significant to the degree that the person is immobilized, a Command Post is set up and several search party members are dispatched to the location with medical and/or survival equipment. A Command Post is a temporary communications system that connects a station on the Whitney Portal Road with the airport, the Sheriff's station, and those on the mountain conducting the search and rescue.

The "best case" scenario is when someone with the injured party is able to locate a Ranger on the Trail. Ideally, the Ranger would have radio contact with the Ranger Station in Lone Pine and would report the problem. That Station would in turn call the Sheriff's Department to dispatch any available rescue unit. It should be emphasized that this chain of events happens very seldom due to limited Ranger contact, and the low probability that a helicopter will be available immediately. Also, most accidents do not happen during ideal conditions. People tend to get hurt during inclement weather, and often it is after sundown. This means there is high wind, overcast skies, and darkness—conditions making it impossible to fly into the area.

Both military and contract helicopters are used for rescues on Mt. Whitney. The Navy, the Highway Patrol, National Parks, and the Forest Service are all called upon to conduct helicopter rescue operations, depending on season and availability. Privately owned helicopters are contracted out of Independence by the Forest Service for firefighting operations, during the summer

> *"Jan got a little beat up on the chute. Search & Rescue saved the day! Thanks"*
> *-7/4/90, Los Angeles, CA*

months. If not out fighting a fire, they may be called upon for Search and Rescue duties. When a helicopter is not available in Independence, the Sheriff's Department may call the California Highway Patrol (CHP) to dispatch a crew from as far away as Fresno. Navy helicopters are another option, and may be dispatched from Lemoore Naval Air Station, China Lake, or Travis Air Force Base. When a hiker is in trouble on the west side of Mt. Whitney, the National Park Service Rangers may call air rescue teams from Kings Canyon or Sequoia. Because of these various resources and the distances involved, there is a wide range in the time it may take for a rescue unit to arrive after a call for help has been made.

The shortest amount of time we have ever seen between an injury and a subsequent rescue is about two hours.
Most rescues take six to eight hours. Some may take from
twelve hours to several days.

Rescues on Mt. Whitney are not like on TV or in a
movie, where help appears to be immediate. Some visitors to
the area have suggested that since they paid for their "ticket" to
hike the Trail (a Permit), they should have access to instant rescue capabilities with all the modern devices

> *"Made it out sick with incredible
> strength & courage"*
> *-6/18/99, MA*

and apparatus available in a big city. What they don't understand is that the Wilderness Act specifies a limitation on mecha-
nized vehicles. There is a fine line and some differences of
opinion about whether a rescue helicopter is in violation by
going into a Wilderness Area.

It has been argued, from a climbers standpoint, that you
cheat people out of an experience by rescuing them. A full
mountain experience includes an acceptance of the "ride," and
people should be obligated to help themselves. No one should
be expected to violate this code by bringing in special equipment. The only proper resource for someone in trouble should
be other climbers who come to help.

> *"[5:30] ...we arrived at Trail Camp....the helicopter
> had already taken off...the person supposedly in
> distress had not wanted to be flown out for medical
> aid. He claimed he could make it on his own."*
> *-Tom LaRocca, "This Year or Never," 7/79*

> *"...many backpackers expect their trips to be peril-free strolls through the woods. If so, they should do their best to achieve that end, by hiking always in sizeable groups on easy, well-marked trails, in temperate weather, rather than courting "adventure," and then demanding to be bailed out when Adventure shows its darker side"*
> *-J. Roblee, 1/12/97*

3. What Happens At The Store

While there are no established rescue capabilities at the Portal, we who have spent time behind the counter know the terrible outcome if someone is left unattended with a minor injury and not taken care of for shock or hypothermia. As we listen to the details being related to us, we are mentally calculating the hours of exposure that have already occurred, and how many more hours it will take for a rescue operation to reach the person. Unfortunately, there are occasions when we realize that the clock has run out.

WHAT WE DO AT THE STORE:

1. Call the Inyo County Sheriff's dispatch at 760-876-5606, rather than 911. A call from a cell phone to 911 connects with the CHP, and we have had trouble with communications. For problems over the crest, call Sequoia/Kings at 209-565-3195.
2. Gather all details: who, what, where, and when.
3. Find out if the party is moving, and if so, which direction (up or down?). Also, consider if they could have made a wrong turn at Trail Crest. Has anybody seen them on "this side" of the mountain? If not, they may be on the west side.
4. Figure out which trail they are on. Which canyon are they

in? Where did they start, and how did it look? We can usually tell if they started up the "true" or "false" (Carillon Drainage) Mountaineer's Route, or most other canyons, if someone can give a description of the terrain.

5.   Receive a call back from a Sheriff, who will talk with the reporting party. They may dispatch a Sheriff to come to the Portal Store for a report and evaluation.

6.   Talk to hikers coming in off the trail to gather news. When we have information such as the color of the person's hat or pack, their gender, age, etc., we can piece together a running report of when the person was seen, where, and how they were doing. This is VERY CRITICAL information. It helps the Sheriff determine whether they are moving, and how fast. Figuring out how long it took them to get from point A to point B will give important clues about where they are now (point C).

7.   Submit a report to the Sheriff, who can then radio for help if determined appropriate, as described above. Next comes the long wait for a search party and/or helicopter to be mobilized. What do we do in the meantime?

Father and son (Doug Sr. and Jr.) have a 2-1/2 mile limit. If we can help, we leave the Store, grab a day pack with supplies, and go. If someone is tired, blistered, beat up from a fall, or has an ankle or knee injury, and they are moving, we take their pack. We give them water, ice, candy, two walking sticks, and talk to them.

Once we went up and a couple was having trouble getting down because the wife had hurt her ankle. The husband would carry her down several hundred feet on his back, leave her on a rock, and then go back and bring down their packs. This was easy to help with; we just took their packs and everyone got down in no time.

• •

E. THE BEARS

"Are there really bears here?" Or how about, "Are there A LOT of bears here?" These questions come up all the time. We don't yet have a baseline of X number of bears per square tree to measure against, so we're not sure how many are "a lot" of bears. People always want to know about the bears, but most folks have a hard time believing what we tell them until they encounter these remarkable animals themselves. We've added this chapter in the second edition, sharing some stories about our own bear experiences and observations.

Hikers are now required to carry their food in a bear resistant container on the Whitney Trail. We expect these will be re-quired state-wide before

> *"Bears ate our car"*
> *-7/2/00, Lancaster, CA*

long. Even if you go where they are not required, using a bear canister is the best way to ensure you will have food to eat, and your camp won't be bothered by bears.

Each Portal campsite has a very small food box to store your supplies. You must clean it out when you check out. The problem is, people are travelling and carrying 6 days' provisions for six people. This might fill two large ice chests, plus a water container and food bag. The campsite food box will only hold about one-fourth of this, so the rest gets stored in someone's car. The car, van, or truck is broken into, the owner is cited, and all the items stored in it are covered with bear saliva, poop and hair.

The campers leave angry, and the next group arrives with their two ice chests, water container, and grocery bags of chips and muffins. The story continues until one day someone has to come and shoot the bear. We can either run out of bears or stop the cycle.

We spend many hours a year trying to show folks the cause and effect of items in their vehicle, and every year we hear the same arguments. "The van was clean! Nothing was in there except—only—just…" "I didn't have time to read the signs." "I saw the broken glass all over but thought it was kids doing the damage" "Do you REALLY have bears here?" "I'm not taking all my stuff out of the car! I'll cover it up with a blanket!" "The ice chest was empty!"

> *"Bears messed with my truck"*
> *-7/25/99, Chino, CA*

We have also watched all the "safe" methods fail—bleach, moth balls, ammonia, pepper, hot sauce, urine, taco seasoning, etc. Once a bear is rewarded by finding food, it will associate a particular sight (ice chest) or smell (white gas) and respond to it.

We now have devised a method to keep your vehicle bear proof. Bring your friend's vehicle. Leave nothing in it. Leave the windows all the way down and the trunk open.

So, what have we learned living with bears for over fifteen seasons? Each bear has a personality. You can fool some of them some of the time, but by the next day they have figured you out. They can move quickly through brush or between cars unnoticed. They follow about the same paths each year, returning to areas where they found food. We know places they return to each day or each year.

They are very polite, and appear hurt if you scold them when they are taking food from cars or tables. Also, they seem to respect territory, and they like recognition. Some come by our sleeping area acting like they want to be seen, and then move on.

Bears move quietly and may appear suddenly anywhere in the area. Kathy Thompson walked out the back door one night, and walked right into a bear hanging out behind the Store. Both of them were very surprised! On another evening, Doug was clearing off a table in the patio area when he realized a bear was standing behind the trees watching to see if any scraps were left from dinner.

Many times we watch from our trailer as bears go along the rock wall past our windows. One year the pattern was to bump the corner of the trailer each time they passed. One night, Earlene

> *"Enjoyed camping & hiking & a bear entered our car & ate our food!"*
> *-7/18/88, San Jacinto, CA*

was sitting on the trailer steps when a bear walked right up to her as if no one was there. "Hey bear," she said, and the animal moved away.

One day, an experienced hiker was at the Store talking about the city folks who don't know how to protect their food. My friend told him to look out the door because a bear was tearing his pack apart as he spoke. The guy thought it was a good joke until he turned around and saw the bear and his pack heading north.

Gene and Jeannine Hauet were camp hosts at the Portal for a long time. We used to share the bear patrol in the area, moving the bears out of the parking lots and campground. There is nothing like seeing a large bear sitting in a new car or van ripping into the boxes of food and drinks that people have left. We saw this happen many times—sometimes several times in one night.

Trunk storage used to be safe, but the bears figured that trick out around 1995. Now when they smell something in the trunk, they break a window, rip the back seat and rear deck apart, and pull the luggage and boxes open one by one to get at the attractant. This is not a pretty picture when the bear's work is complete. Then a Ranger will issue a citation.

Don't stay in the wilderness for a week if you are careless with food storage in your car. Here's the scenario: the day you leave, a bear breaks into the vehicle. Each additional day the bear and its buddies visit your car, removing more items. At times the roof becomes a picnic table for mass bear feedings.

> *My friend was freaked when she saw a bear!"*
> *-7/1/00, Los Angeles, CA*

This problem is now being addressed by a new policy—your car will not only be ticketed, it will be towed off the mountain.

People ask us why bears don't come into the Store at night. The answer is simple: we put up the "Closed" sign!

Actually, what we do is a long and continuous process to control lack of access to food or trash. We close the kitchen one hour before the Store closes. We clean the entire Store and kitchen. We have no trash cans outside. We clear the tables and hose the area down. The food is stored in the interior of the building, away from windows. We inspect the area about 30 minutes after we close and then again about 11:00 p.m. to make sure no one has left packs or trash on the tables. We try to keep the shower room locked because people could leave trash in there after we close, and bears would go in after the trash.

The camp hosts, Fish and Game staff, local sheriffs, Forest Service personnel, and the Whitney Store gang spend many hours each year making sure the bears have a safe season with no access to human food. We know from observing these bears that diligent 100% food control works. Only WE the PEOPLE can control the food cycle.

At times it may seem OK to leave things out in your camp, or out of your car. Please understand that these slight breaches of food control can lead to a season of broken windows, lost packs, and in the final analysis, the death of a bear.

We remember one year when a bear became aggressive in search of human food. We moved the bear into the forest, and as Doug walked back through the campground, he passed three campsites with food left unattended on the table. The camp host had talked to these campers. Signs are all over the area. Each table has a warning about bears, and proper food storage lockers are provided. The next morning, the bear was shot.

Vehicle damage inflicted by a bear seeking food
(photo courtesy of Gene & Jeannine Hauet)

Sky Pilot (Polemonium eximium) above Iceberg Lake
(photo by Marcyn Del Clements)

F. THE WILDLIFE

The way we look at it:

So what do you call them? Real simple—if they walk they're animals; if they fly they're birds, bats, or bees; if they bloom they're flowers—and the rest we call scrub. After spending most of our time outdoors, and in most of the Western U.S., we have observed that if you call a duck a duck, someone will help you with, "No, it's a ___." This holds true with flowers, animals, rocks, dirt, water, moss, algae, etc. So we didn't want to spend a lot of time on this, as there are good books on all these areas. And, every few years, new books will appear with the "final interpretation." So please don't feel put out if someone asks you what something is called, and you don't know.

> *"Wunderschon"*
> *-7/17/99, Switzerland*

If you are out and about looking, smelling, feeling, listening, and even tasting, you have been touched by your experience, and the more times you expose yourself to the outs and abouts, you expand your reference database. Then you will start to see the color changes, the leaf structures, the number of needles on the pines, and the color and detail of the rock formations.

Our view is that it's a lifelong process of exposure. So don't limit yourself to what exists in written material. What you see and experience in this visit is filling your storage banks. You

81

can be rewarded through the realization that we pass through life as a magnet, and we can attract or repel our surroundings by how we process what our experiences are. We talk with many people who just go up the trail and down, getting to the summit as the primary objective. This is good, but if you expand your expectations into a sightseeing trip rather than simply a challenge, the encounter is very different.

Some people ask, "How do you stay in this canyon all these years?" Well, we could go on about the friends we have made over the years, the easy lifestyle, the joy of cleaning up the store every day, etc. But honestly, every day we experience something new. We know that at the beginning of the year when few campers are in the canyon, wildlife is all about. We see it during the main season as night closes in, and human activity slows down. Back it comes each year, with different snow levels, and different times of winter arrival.

> *"Great trail, beautiful scenery"*
> *-5/28/99, No. Vancouver, B.C., Canada*

The temperatures of May and June will bring a host of flowers and grasses which will bring the deer, birds, squirrels, chipmunks, mice, and more. From a different perspective, it appears the animals have adapted to a peaceful co-existence, moving slightly away from the bustling crowds, and appearing again at quieter times.

We are including a list of birds and flowers that were experienced on several hikes by Marcyn Del Clements. (See Appendix D.) These are shared for an introduction. One can add the scrub, ground cover, and plant life that will display for limited amounts of time and frequency.

• •

G. TOILET TROUBLES

The essence of a wilderness experience includes going
without some things, including a comfortable, private bathroom
with a flushing toilet. Since Mt. Whitney is THE most visited
wilderness area in the Sierra, it naturally follows that lots of
people have a need to relieve themselves at the Whitney Portal
and along the Trail. This has caused some problems.

1. Portal Facilities

At this writing, there are four pit toilets at the Portal.
Two are in the day parking area southwest of the pond, and are
only open during the season (May through October). The other
two are at the overflow parking lot, and stay open all year long.

Several years ago, a truck was pumping out the tanks
when someone thought they smelled and saw a human body, or
parts of one, in the muck. With some alarm, they asked the
Store People to summon the Sheriff. After a great deal of
hubbub and poking about, the analysis was made. Some visitor
had stuffed a jacket into the latrine. The garment became
inflated with gas and waste, giving it the appearance of a torso.
In addition, someone else had cleaned a deer and disposed of
the entrails in the toilet. The blood and guts made a terrific
smell, and a colorful decoy. Everyone was greatly relieved that
an autopsy would not have to be performed.

2. Trail Toilets

For a number of years, the Forest Service has maintained solar toilets at two locations on the Whitney Trail: Outpost Camp and Trail Camp. (The Summit latrine belongs to the National Park Service.) The term "solar" refers to the disposal method whereby solid waste is aerated, dried, and then removed. Unfortunately, many hikers do not follow the posted instructions, and the results have been disastrous. The drying process is slowed down by urine content, and at times the toilets cannot handle the heavy volume of peak season use. This makes it necessary for the Forest Service to close them periodically.

> "We _loved_ the solar toilets!"
> -7/20/90, Gainesville, FL

Any time the toilets are closed, "meadow muffins" are deposited on the ground nearby, along with used toilet paper, causing a tremendous environmental and social mess. Good trail hygiene dictates that excrement be buried six inches deep, but the rock-hard surfaces at Trail Camp and the summit make this a real challenge. Locked toilets and poop -covered surroundings have made some people angry. The toilets have been vandalized more than once, costing taxpayers thousands of dollars.

> "Talk to rangers to keep more
> T.P. on hand in restrooms"
> -9/2/90, Reno, NV

One creative solution that allows each hiker to be responsible for his or her contribution is the use of a "kitty litter" bag for collecting feces and packing it out of the wilderness.

While this may seem distasteful, it could help tremendously in the preservation of this wilderness area. Since 1996, "Nature Calls" bags have been available at the trailhead on a voluntary basis for hikers on the Mountaineers Route. They are also dispensed at the Store for people who want to use them. Special disposal cans are at the bottom of the trail for used bags.

This complex set of problems does not have an easy solution. It is one of the greatest, if not THE greatest, challenge in maintaining the area. New methods of disposal are being introduced regularly. We strongly advise all hikers to follow posted instructions carefully. Please understand that you are expected to pack out ALL your garbage. The toilets are NOT to be used as trash receptacles.

Solar Toilet at Trail Camp
(photo courtesy of Russell Simon)

It is not the number of visitors that impact this area as much as the individual actions of each one. Please do your part to help the Forest Service and the National Park Service deal with human waste on the Mt. Whitney Trail.

"Take a dump on the top"
-7/5/88, Bakersfield, CA

Toilet at the Summit: "The Throne"
(please close the door!)

•   •

H. WEATHER

It was 92 degrees in LA when you left; it was 100 degrees in Lone Pine. It is 75 degrees at the Portal and it will be about 51 degrees on the summit during a summer day. Now add the possibility of wind, sleet, rain and lightning. We notice a mood effect on people during bad weather days. You need to decide on what your experience level will allow you to do.

No one can tell you what the weather will be like in a week or two, or even tomorrow. We suggest that you don't even bother to ask because it will only give you false hopes if someone tells you what you want to hear.

"Too much snow!"
-5/18/91, Oceanside, CA

What we look at:

How much sleet or snow is there, and what time will it freeze in the afternoon? If the storm is moving out/in, how high will the wind be? We watch the sky for sun dogs and devil dogs. These ice crystals in the atmosphere indicate a cold storm is in the area and could bring snow within hours or several days. It is very hard to tell exactly when this will happen, so when we go out we assume it will happen every day. And when it starts, we just head back home. Storms are brought in by wind and taken out by wind. If the wind starts, with clouds moving in and building up, it could rain, turn to sleet and snow, and continue falling. If the wind stops, expect the storm to stay in the area. When the wind starts again, the storm will move.

We had about three days of pouring rain one season, where everybody was waiting to go up each day. The people coming down were giving detailed reports on how heavy the rain was, how deep it was running in the trail, where it was turning to snow, how windy it was, etc. We had a display showing every kind of foul weather gear on the market. The only thing keeping people dry was the bright yellow "rubber ducky" suit—something that any well-dressed, serious mountaineer would never buy or be seen wearing.

> *"Windy, chest-high snow bluffs*
> *—a challenge to find the trail"*
> *-10/29/00, Earth*

No one should go into the higher elevations during possible lightning storms. And when the area is covered with clouds, it is impossible to see the thunderheads building or the distant lightning flashes warning the direction of the storm. Most storms will drop sleet or snow on the area above Trail Crest any time during the summer. Your summer may be three months long, but our summer is short—July plus the first three weeks of August.

Always watch for lightning. High winds, falling trees and branches, rockslides and flash floods are very common in the narrow canyons. Also, during the winter runoff season, streams will swell at night due to melting action all day and travel time to get to lower elevations. If you need to do a stream crossing, plan to do it early in the morning.

Temperature extremes are common in the mountains. We had a 43-degree drop in about a hour several years ago.

At higher elevations, once the sun goes down, expect the temperature to drop considerably. Above the tree line it's just plain cold every night. At Trail Camp in August, nights are in the 30's or 40's, but can easily dip to the 20's. The last thing you want to do is be tired, hungry, cold, and still have ten miles to go after dark.

We see a lot of nights in July and August when slower hikers get up to Trail Crest at 5:00 or 6:00 p.m. and insist on going to the summit. This puts them back at Trail Crest in the dark with the cold setting in. Just whip out your pocket calculator and figure the experience going down. This is obviously courting disaster, and brings on what we call the "Saturday Night Special."

From an Expert:

Shawn Trueman, a meteorologist who is familiar with the Sierras, offers these tips for late spring to early autumn weather:

- The earlier in the day the cumulus clouds form over the mountains, the greater the likelihood of showers/thunderstorms that day. The precipitation type in these showers and thunderstorms may be rain, snow, snow or ice pellets, and/or hail

- The clouds almost always form first over the crest and then expand east and west. However, the clouds can also form over the Great Western Divide (a range of the Sierra west of the main crest) and move eastward.

- Want to learn more? Search the Internet for upper-level wind data, and check the wind direction at 500 millibars (about 18,000 feet above sea level) at nearby stations such as Reno and Mercury, Nevada. If upper-

89

air winds are from the south or southeast over the Sierra, there is a high probability of showers and thunderstorms. High winds from the southwest indicate that showers are not likely.

- Still curious? Search again for water-vapor satellite imagery. If you can see white over the Sierra, there is a high likelihood of showers and thunderstorms. Conversely, if the water-vapor imagery is dark (black) over the area, storms are less likely.
- From mid-autumn to mid-spring, the storm track brings low-pressure systems into California from the Pacific.

> *"Bloody Hell it's cold"*
> *-9/26/89, Ballymena, N. Ireland*

Two-foot icicles along the Trail

90

Max Newbold modeling a rain poncho

Physical Fitness Isn't Everything
Eight Factors (other than physical fitness)
Contributing to your Ability to
Climb Mt. Whitney

1. **Genetic Factors - Size of heart, lungs, arteries, skull, brain**

2. **Altitude Acclimation - Percentage of red blood cells (at what altitude do you live; have you spent some time at the Portal? It takes about 3 months to acclimate completely)**

3. **Mental and Emotional Expectations - Degree of self-confidence, tenacity, determination to reach summit**

4. **Level of Tolerance - Threshold for pain, nausea, heights**

5. **Weather - Temperature, precipitation, ice or snow on trail**

6. **Medication - Use of pain relievers, inhalers, diamox**

7. **Nutrition - Carbohydrates and sugars vs. fat and proteins**

8. **Preparation - Adequate clothing, equipment and supplies**

• •

I. YOUR SUCCESS FACTORS

The Three Big Questions:

We can ask three questions and establish a fair guess about how people will do on the hike:
1. Do you diet?
2. How much water/electrolytes did you drink the past several days?
3. Have you ever hiked over 12,000 feet?

1. Do you diet?
If you diet, and you haven't change your eating habits several weeks before this hike, your body may not have enough stored energy. Also, you might not bring the 4,000-6,000 calories to replace what you are using on the hike.

What we do: Eat as you hike to keep fueling your body.
What we eat: Gu, Clif Bars, honey packets, candy, bread, cheese, jerky, pop tarts, nuts, trail mix.

> *"Hiked from Badwater Valley, Baby!"*
> *-7/4/99, Reno, NV*

2. How much water/electrolytes did you drink the past several days?
Water consumption is important days before the hike. People who train for the Badwater Race (from Death Valley to

93

Whitney Portal in July) exercise in heat to adjust their bodies for processing large amounts of liquid.

What we do: Drink 4-6 quarts of water each day for several days prior to the hike. The day before, drink 4 quarts of Gookinaid. On the day of the hike, drink 4-5 quarts of Gookinaid from the Portal to Trail Camp. Purification method: Iodine (Potable Aqua) tablets – 2 per quart plus Gookinaid. This replaces the chemicals you lose.

By eating and drinking regularly, you replace liquid and calories as you go. Doug says: "I **never** sweat or breath hard. If I feel my body getting warm or flush, I slow down. Pushing your body only starts the failure cycle – rapid loss of hydration and energy, i.e. cramps, soreness, muscle fatigue and hitting that point of exhaustion and dehydration.

> *"It was a tough climb"*
> *-6/30/88, Barstow, CA*
>
> *"A cinch"*
> *-6/30/88, Mt. Shasta, CA*

How do you know what your body can do? Short, hard training will prepare your body and mind for a short, hard event. You can condition for the experience, but…look at the old, overweight construction worker who can go up and down the mountain with no problem. Wearing a pair of Broughans, bib overalls, and a cotton sweatshirt, he probably never heard of the brand name boots or gear we see on the trail.

This person has developed long term endurance by being on his feet 10-12 hours a day. His work includes pushing, shoving, twisting, turning, and lifting, with short bursts of high energy output followed with rest. He does this day after day, knowing that if he does not take care of the machine and control the output, he will not last all day on the job.

If labor-intensive workers failed at the rate of hikers, they would not be employed, due to lack of ability to work all day every day. Their working conditions may include heat, cold, rain, snow, wind, noise, odors, etc. This makes for a total mind/body adjustment. So if you plan to train, add to your cookbook some 10-15 mile hikes and see if you can stay alert, enjoying yourself. Try to get to the level that you can do this nonstop or at least by company rules: 15 minutes morning break, 30 minutes lunch break, and 15 minutes afternoon break.

> *"After seven months of preparation of mind, gear, & body, (and climbing any other mountains we could) we did it"*
> *-10/15/00, Cayce, SC*

3. Have you ever hiked over 12,000 feet?

If someone has hiked above 12,000 feet, this tells us they have not just been in California doing short coastal hikes up local mountains. They will have experienced the effect of ice-sun-wind-cold-heat-snow above tree line, and maybe learned to breath a little differently and what to expect. Above tree line, we call it the moonscape: rocks, rocks, and more rocks. Now one must look for visual relief. Look to the macro views—far away valleys, mountains beyond, and lakes below. Enjoy the tiny streams, soaring birds, and the chance of the high altitude flowers: sky pilot, and alpine gold. Savor the glimpses of rosy finches and the pesky marmots.

Around 11,000-12,000 feet, most people who are ill prepared physically or mentally turn back. The hikers who try to carry a 50-60 pound pack to Trail Camp will see a very slow go from above Mirror Lake to Trail Camp. Doug's motto is, "One can never carry enough stuff you don't need."

This short three-fold inquiry can give us a window into what may predict the outcome. But we also believe the most important input is if people are honest with themselves and follow sound judgement. If they are prepared mentally and physically, they will make it to the summit and back. Our experience is that those who make it are not always the extreme fitness type.

Your Mental and Physical Preparation

We remember one day we were talking about a runner from Ridgecrest who went up and down in 5.5 hours. A customer said he had run marathons in 2:40, and it took him over 7 hours to go up and down Whitney—he didn't believe it was possible to do it in less. What he didn't

> *"I think I can, I think I can, give or take a little"*
> *-7/11/00, Des Moines, IA*

understand was that running a 2:40 marathon does NOT prepare you mentally for such a climb as the Whitney Trail.

What can we learn from this? Ask yourself this question: Do you really want to make it to the summit? We're not talking about the approach that some folks take, where they will force themselves at all cost to get to the top. You need to think in terms of enjoying yourself. Think about it this way: Will I see five new flowers, five new trees, and five types of wildlife? Or will I see only the dirt and rock on the trail two steps in front of me?

The first time up Whitney can be doomed by anxiety. People worry about "what if" this or that, "where are we?" and "how much farther?" They see people passing them and notice some piece of gear ("look, they have one of those, I should have one too"). They fall into the "should have" frame of mind: If only the weather was hotter/colder, not raining or wind blowing.

Let's assume that you have followed a training schedule; gotten rid of excess pack weight; eaten heartily and conditioned your body to process liquid and energy; and you have gone on several long walks. The main trail to the summit is a walk, just like you would take in a mall or golf course, but less threatening. No one is likely to rob you, and you won't be caught in a crossfire of gang activity, or be struck by a flying golf club or ball.

> *"Try acclimatizing"*
> *-6/24/00, Seattle, WA*

Get to the Portal several days ahead of your hike. Take a drive to Horseshoe Meadows and walk around the area. The parking lot is 10,000+ feet altitude, and walking to the first lake gets you to about 11,000 in about three miles. This walk will let you experience the elevation, the dryness of the air, and approximate how the Whitney Trail is to the summit. Practice breathing and pace.

We strongly urge people to use (two) walking sticks. We know they work and will make the down walk a lot more risk free by taking the shock

> *"It was hell and heaven put together"*
> *-8/4/99, San Fernando Valley, CA*

off your knees, ankles, and lower body. With practice, you can use the sticks to pull yourself up the trail. Now you have transferred some of the work off your legs and put your arms/ upper body to work instead of just taking them along on the ride.

Let's go over some numbers that float around the climbing scene. At 14,000 feet, the air pressure is approximately 80% of that at sea level. You also lose 30% of your strength due to altitude. So, how do you recoup these losses? One good way is by taking weight off your pack. Carry a go-lite type pack—ounces, not pounds, of dead weight. Hydrate and energize your body up to the 14,000' level. Use the walking sticks and your upper body strength. Use the "pressure breath" technique—a strong exhale with a "pop" to get old air out of the lungs. If you don't clear your lungs of all the stale air, you don't have sufficient volume for fresh oxygen-carrying air that you badly need.

> *"Well worth the pain & fear"*
> *-6/14/99, San Diego, CA*

C.O.E. = Conservation Of Energy. Walk slowly; prevent profuse sweating and rapid breathing. Your body sweats to cool it down, and gasping for air says you're lacking oxygen. Sweat is taking liquid and chemicals from your body, and rapid breathing is also sapping vital moisture from your body.

Look at the winner of marathons. He or she is used up at the end—sometimes cramping, vomiting, or falling to the ground exhausted. Now take that same person and do the marathon in six hours, replenishing liquid and energy as they go, and transferring about 30% of the work to the upper body by using poles to pull themselves forward. Now when this person crosses the finish line, they should look about the same as they did when they started. Did they win? Did they see , smell, sense, or touch the world that day? Which is more important?

When we talk about slow pace, this will be different for everyone. But using the body as a guide, you will adjust to what's comfortable. A general rule we see is about 1 mile per hour up and a little faster down, for day hikers. For overnight hikers, the pack weight is the limiting factor. As people buy more security and gadgets to play with, they must stop to rest and recover from the load.

Look at the process as simple physics—a certain level of work is required to carry a given load over a particular distance. Therefore, the less load you carry, the less work is required. From a mechanical viewpoint, a car gets rid of heat through a radiator; it gets fuel from a gas tank; its surfaces that are subject to wear are cooled and lubricated by special oil; and air is forced into its combustion chamber to facilitate production of energy. Now, overload any mechanical device within the car, and watch it fail if any one of the components are lacking.

> *"First timers—we came, we saw, it kicked our ass"*
> *-10/4/99, Harbor City, CA*

How Long Will It Take?

The most frequently-asked question in the Store is:

> **"How long does it take a "normal" person in fairly good health, and in fairly good shape, to get up to the top?"**

Why do so many people ask this question? Probably because they want to know if they are above or below average. Someone will usually dispute whatever answer is given. If the Store People tell them it takes five hours, they argue that's too fast. If the answer of 15 hours is given, they say their friend did it in 11 hours.

The reader must realize there is much more to "getting up to the top" than being in good shape physically. Marathon runners have attempted the summit and failed. On the other hand, there is an amazingly steady stream of hikers who do reach the summit in one or two days without being physically fit. This is because there are a number of variables other than physical strength that contribute to each person's speed and success along their way to the top of Mt. Whitney.

Recorded in the Guest Book is a timed record for the Mountaineer's Route of 2:08:34 to the summit, and 3:23:01 round trip by Marty Hornick on September 29, 1991. This route is steeper and more direct than the main trail. A distance of 3.4 miles was wheeled in 2001. Marty's record stood for over a decade, but it was recently toppled. Jason Lakey went up and down the Mountaineer's Route in 3:10 on August 24, 2002.

Vernon Morrison doesn't run it for speed, but one day he went up and down the Main Trail twice, both times in just over 3 hours. He thinks if he ran it for time, he could cut it by 20 minutes, giving a record of 2:50 or so. Someday someone will come up and do it like a marathon. An obtainable record could be somewhere around 2:30 or 2:35. It's shorter than the 26-mile marathon run.

The Whitney Trail can be done in five hours or less; most people need more time.

> *"Departed at 2:30 pm -*
> *Returned 8:00 - 5 hr 30 min"*
> *-7/16/88, San Diego, CA*
>
> *"9.5 hrs."*
> *-8/13/88, Austria*
>
> *"11 hrs to top and back (73 yrs)"*
> *-8/8/88, Miami, FL*
>
> *"17 hrs up & back???!!!"*
> *-8/22/88, Berkeley, CA*

•••••••••••••••••••••••••••••

J. MOONLIGHT HIKING

Let's talk about the moonlight hike—when to leave, what to expect, and how many days before and after the full moon you can do it. Climbing the mountain at night has the potential for a unique and very beautiful wilderness experience. There is greater solitude, and moonlight shining on the granite walls is truly awesome.

Plan to arrive at the Portal early in the day so you can spend the afternoon resting

> *"Bright Moonlight!!!"*
> *-8/12/90, Hacienda Heights, CA*

and adjusting to the area. A few days in the family campground would be ideal, making the full moon trip part of a vacation. Also, this gives you time to gather information about weather and trail conditions from hikers coming down off the mountain.

Timing: Expect to leave the Portal area around 12:00-12:30 a.m. If you leave before midnight, you need an overnight permit. Go slow and steady. It will be cool, and the higher up you go, the colder it will get. As you get sleepier, you will slow down, so watch your time between key landmarks. Outpost Camp is 1/3 of the way; Trail Camp is halfway; and Trail Crest is 2/3. The trick is to keep moving, reaching Trail Crest at sunup. That is an experience in itself. Complete the last section as the sun rises in the east. This should put you at the summit around 7:00-8:00 a.m. Most mornings, this will allow you to be the first to sign the register.

When to Go: You can see well enough about three days before and after the full moon. This gives you a window of about seven days per month. July and August are the best choices. You can try this in June if all the snow is off the trail, but most years it is still too cold to do the hike at night. Any melt water will freeze and make the trip a safety call. A thin layer of "black ice" forms over the rocks. It is very hard to see, or distinguish from running water. In a dry year, if the weather holds, you can do it in September.

> *"Do it at night"*
> *-6/27/92, Bremerton, WA*

What to Take: Bring a flashlight, batteries, and bulbs. The section of the Trail under tree cover will be dark. Wear and/or carry enough layers of clothing to keep comfortable at around 10 degrees. This includes long pants, thermal type undies, gloves, headgear and warm boots. Food, stove, snacks, etc. are about the same as a day hike, except that since it's colder, you may want more food. As "early morning syndrome" sets in, some coffee, tea, or hot chocolate will help. However, many nights it's so cold you don't feel like stopping.

When to Stop: If a wind/storm comes up, do not continue. Head back down. If the wind is blowing at lower elevations, expect what we call the "hawk" at upper elevations. This is wind that zaps all your body heat and is so strong that forward motion stops and balance is hard to maintain. Remember, for all practical purposes, Trail Crest **is** the summit—you can see into the back country, you are at 13,777 elevation, and you are within a stone's throw of the hut—well, almost.

> *"Just missed reaching the summit—back next year for a rematch!"*
> *-9/16/00, Palo Alto, CA*

III. ALONG THE WAY

A. LIFE AT THE TOP

Celebrations

The top of Mount Whitney is a singular place. Upon reaching the summit, a pause for reflection and self-congratulations is in order. For most people, snapping some photos is enough to mark the moment. However, folks have done more unusual things to commemorate their conquest of the Mountain. A number of couples have become engaged while at the summit. Some have celebrated birthdays, complete with cake and champagne. Many cell phone calls have been placed.

We should take a moment to remind all visitors that it is a federal offense to remove ANYTHING from this very special site. If everyone took one piece of anything, it would soon cause deterioration. Please preserve the place for your grandchildren to enjoy when their turn comes to climb Mount Whitney. Besides, you don't want your pack to weigh any more than it already does, so please don't pick up souvenirs.

> *"I felt like singing out a thousand alleluias. What a tremendous and overpowering feeling it was to know that I was on top of the world, at least here in the continental United States"*
> *-Tom LaRocca, "This Year Or Never," 7/79*

Upon reaching the summit of Mount Whitney for the first time, John Muir found a half dollar with the inscription, "Whoever finds this is welcome to it—Carl Rabe" (spelling has been edited). John Muir left the money there, but someone else took Mr. Rabe up on his offer.

Money—you shouldn't expect to need any at the summit, but some entrepreneurial folks have sold hot coffee, beer, and wine for outrageous prices up there. Others have charged $50 for a call from their cell phone. The Guest Book at the Store is replete with comments which jokingly suggest business improvements for the peak: a fast food store, an elevator, a tram, and many more. While there is no zoning atop Mt. Whitney (yet) for commercial endeavors, it has been called "another roadside tourist attraction"

> *"Get rid of the Air Force Jets!"*
> *-8/15/89, Concord, MA*

along the "hikers highways"—the John Muir and Pacific Crest Trails.

Evidence of civilization has taken to the skies of Whitney in recent years as fighter jets from nearby military bases practice maneuvers over the area. To some hikers, the vapor trails are beautiful to behold, especially when tinted with colors of sunrises or sunsets. Others, however, see them simply as a detraction from the visual environment. Noise pollution is another issue. The roar of jets as they zoom the summit or break the sound barrier is a jarring reminder of the stresses of city life. At times they fly quite low, sending the roar echoing off canyon walls, terrifying animals and upsetting campers who come to the mountains to find some peace and quiet.

While at the summit, hikers are often treated to a spectacular airshow. Some argue that such invasion of the wilderness should be outlawed. Others find it an awesome sight which augments the thrill and excitement of attaining the top of the Mountain.

Sometimes gliders can be seen, soaring like silent giant white birds, hundreds of feet above.

> *"A jet fighter ... came buzzing over us with only a few yards to spare—then climbed up until he was only a tiny speck, and bore down on us in a series of slow rolls, sweeping only 25 feet above the stone hut on the summit, and diving out of sight into the Owens Valley below!"*
> *-Bob Bacon, 7/94*

The Hut

The most noticeable landmark on the summit is the stone hut. For today's visitors, the amazing thing about this building is that it was constructed before helicopters were invented. When you think about what you just went through to haul yourself up to the summit, you can appreciate, to a small degree, the task of hauling up materials and completing construction with 1908-1909 tools and technology. This feat, sponsored by the Smithsonian Institution, was performed by Gustave F. Marsh of Lone Pine (See Appendix B, "The Highest House in America," p. 217). He also engineered the early trail to the summit. Fortunately, he had the use of pack animals.

Oscar Bernhardt and mules in front of hut on top of Mt. Whitney
(photo from Eastern California Museum collection)

David Moreau stands next to door of summit hut
(photo by Roger Moreau)

Considering the weather and temperature changes this little building has been exposed to, one must appreciate the quality of engineering and workmanship that went into its construction. Not only has it held up well, it is pleasant to look at. Take a moment to admire its solidity. Mr. Marsh obviously took pride in his work. Dean Prewitt did some restoration work on the shelter for the Forest Service, and the door was rebuilt by Lew Chrispen of Lone Pine. Half the hut is closed to visitors. Please be respectful of this building; do not use it as an "outhouse," and remember to close the door so it won't fill up with snow. People have used it as a shelter for sleeping on the summit. We do not recommend this.

> *"Our son was killed by lightning in the hut at the peak 7/14/90"*
> *-6/10/91, Tucson, AZ*

PLEASE HEED THE WARNING SIGNS ABOUT LIGHTNING!

A hiker was killed in 1990 while taking shelter in the hut during a storm. Others have died at the summit from lightning strikes, beginning with Byrd Surby in 1904. If you notice any impending storm activity, hear buzzing or humming sounds, or sense a lot of electricity in the air, DO NOT STAY ON THE SUMMIT! If you are heading toward the hut, do not continue up the trail to the summit if thunderheads are building over the area and people coming down tell you of electrical charges in the air. Lightning is a hazard all along the ridge, and even down to Trail Camp.

Pros & Cons: Sleeping on the Summit

Pros:
- There is adequate space for camping
- If the restroom is open, your bathroom needs are met
- You will have spent the night on the highest peak in the contiguous US.
- You will become closer friends with others who are doing the same thing

Cons:
- There is no water (unless you gather snow and melt it)
- It is very cold at night, no matter what time of year
- If the restroom is closed, you'll need your "kitty litter" bag (there is no soil in which to bury waste)
- You probably won't get much sleep
- If a storm arrives, you'll be in danger of lightning strikes unless you pack up and hike down in the dark—in the rain/snow
- If any kind of problem develops (hypothermia, leg injury, heart attack, etc.), there will be NO HELP AVAILABLE

Sleeping on the Summit

Each year some people choose to spend a night on the summit. You need to evaluate the pros and cons before you decide to do this (see chart on opposite page).

The authors do not recommend spending the night on the summit due to the Cons listed on this chart. However, we realize there is a certain thrill to it, and adventurers will continue to camp out at the top, if for no other reason than to be able to tell their friends about it. All we can say is, be careful, and use "common sense."

"Slept on Whitney 8/13—fantastic!"
-8/14/88, So. Pasadena, CA

"Horrible night on top"
-7/28/91, Groveland, CA

"Slept on Whitney. Freezing—but the sunrise & set are beautiful!!!"
-9/22/00, San Francisco, CA

Bob Rockwell at the summit 9-27-02—his 94th ascent.
(photo courtesy of Bob Rockwell)

• •

B. RETURN VISITS

It is our observation that about 90% of the people who climb Mt. Whitney have

> *"The earth in its splendor declares the Glory of the Lord!"*
> *-8/27/99, Germany*

what we would call a "spiritual experience." There is something about the area that draws people back again, once they have been here. We have seen people who came to the Portal 20, 30, or more years ago, and are back to fulfill a promise they made to themselves. We also see some of the same people coming back year after year, heeding the call of the Mountain. One older gentleman we know of has climbed it every year, doing it in one day, for many years—an annual pilgrimage.

> *"Magnificent! I'll be back to climb someday!"*
> *-8/8/93, Hermosa Beach, CA*

Bob Rockwell recently commemorated 50 years of climbing Mount Whitney. He provided us with a list of milestone climbs:

- May 24, 1952 - First ascent, age 16
- August 21, 1956 - First full moon ascent
- July 26, 1966 - Family hike to Lone Pine Lake with wife and two sons (ages 2 and 4).
- August 1, 1972 - First time up Mountaineer's Route. Took 10-year-old son (10th ascent)

- December 25, 1973 - Christmas rescue of a climber on East Buttress
- May 20, 1974 - 12th ascent, 101 years minus 1 day after Muir's climb of the Mountaineer's Route
- May 15, 1983 - 25th ascent
- August 5, 1995 - 50th ascent
- February 22, 1997 - 59th ascent (had now climbed it in every month)
- July 13, 1997 - Climbed my age (61st ascent at age 61)
- April 1, 2000 - 75th ascent
- December 31, 2000 - Last climb of the old millennium - 81st ascent
- May 24, 2002 - 50th anniversary of my first climb, and my 89th ascent, age 66

Bob Rockwell personally endorsed gift certificates he handed out to all those who joined him for the 50th anniversary of his first climb

Some people happen by once just to car camp, and then vow to return for the climb. The Guest Book contains hundreds of entries that essentially say, "I'll be back," or "I'm back." Another phenomenon we notice is younger generations of families rediscovering the Whitney Experience of their progenitors. One family visited the Store to tell us this was

"Grandpa's Mountain." They had come here to pay tribute to him after

he had passed away. We see people with childhood memories of camping here, or visiting a Portal cabin, who have returned to bring their own children and introduce them to the area. Some have even been named "Whitney" after the mountain.

For some people who are sick or physically unfit, Mt. Whitney has provided a goal and a motivation to overcome their health problems. They make a promise to get well, or get in shape, and come back to climb the Trail. A lot of them do. This is one of the rewards of being at the Store, because we usually hear about these personal victories.

We have known of double amputees and polio victims who completed not only the Whitney Trail, but the John Muir

"I'll stay here in 9-9-99"
-8/8/88, Mexico

"On our 5th annual family trip"
-7/25/96, Encinitas, CA

"My first but not last!"
-8/10/88, Norfolk, England

"Promised the kids 12 yrs ago we would do this and we did. We'll be back!"
-7/31/88, Cloverdale, CA

"#5"
-6/24/89, Bethesda, MD

"Came back after many years"
-8/6/93, La Mesa, CA

> "We'll be back"
> -6/5/88, San Diego, CA
>
> "Great! Waited 33 years for this"
> -8/21/93, Ridgecrest, CA
>
> "Sick as a dog but still lovin life,
> be back next year"
> -9/2/93, Hanalei, HI

Trail. We have seen people who were diagnosed with one disease or another and were not expected to live long. Mt. Whitney has infused them with a will to recover and a determination to climb it before they die. Some of them make it. We have also met older people who climbed the Mountain when they were younger, and have come back to ponder and reflect on the experience. Although most are no longer able to reach the summit, they take satisfaction in the memory of their past climbing experiences.

A lot of people have passed through the area over the years, and each carries unique memories. Some remember working at the store when they were kids. Others remember when the trailhead was at the west end of the parking lot. Many remember when a permit was not required for this trail, and it was climbed by more than 4,000 people on busy summer weekends. Some remember when pack animals

> "It was beautiful in '69. Hope
> for the best now (age 66)"
> -9/17/88, Los Angeles, CA

were used. One visitor showed us the spot where he was born—in the back of the Store!

Once you have come to Mt. Whitney, chances are you will come back. There is something more than the water, the air, or the granite, that speaks to our inner selves. It seems to cast a spell upon us all, and we are drawn back again and again to renew our spirits. No matter what religion or "non-religion" you believe in, we hope you feel this wonderful "whatever-it-is" and have a desire to return. Be sure to sign in at the Store when you do!

> *"After 25 yrs of coming here, it's still beautiful!"*
> *-8/14/88, Yorba Linda, CA*

To sum it up: a quote from former cabin owner Tom LaRocca from his account, "This Year or Never" (Appendix A, page 195) which he wrote in 1979 after his first ascent of Mt. Whitney at age 58:

> I have often been asked the question: would you do it again? My answer is definitely in the affirmative, for I know now that each time I climb the highest peak in the [continental] United States it will be a thrilling and spiritually rewarding journey.
>
> I began with the thought of doing it once in my lifetime—of achieving it being a this-year-or-never-proposition. I know now that climbing Mt. Whitney is too wonderful to remain just a one-time event in my memory. I want to do it again, because I know that each trip will offer different sights, new experiences, and a chance for me to feel once again the awesome power that comes with being on top of the world.
>
> -Tom LaRocca, "This Year Or Never," 7/79

> *"Fulfillment of lifetime dream!"*
> *-8/21/88, Cerritos, CA*

Three generations on the summit: August 3, 2002
L-R: Megan Heublein (20), Colleen Heublein (47),
Margaret Davis (80)

Tom Davidson on the summit: July 11, 2002
A "survivor" at age 54, Tom has suffered two heart attacks
and lives with chronic lymphocytic leukemia.

•••••••••••••••••••••••••••

C. SPECIAL OCCASIONS

Climbing Mt. Whitney is a special occasion in itself. However, when combined with another milestone in life, it augments the event significantly. The most common celebration we see is birthdays. If you were born somewhere between June and October, this is one way you can celebrate getting older while staying young. Many people come here for those very special birthdays such as number 40, 50, and so on.

> *"Tomorrow's my 80th birthday. Celebrating on the trail!"*
> *-8/28/93, Los Angeles, CA*
>
> *"Celebrated my 35th Birthday, 12 hrs 15 min. The greatest challenge. Love it"*
> *-8/16/88, Los Angeles, CA*

Standing on the summit gives you the perspective that time doesn't really matter, and that your life is small and great all at once.

> *"3 generations on top at one time!"*
> *-8/27/88, CA*

We meet a lot of amazing and inspiring people, including those who face serious health challenges. Climbing the Mountain is a significant achievement for healthy folks. A

> *"We celebrated our 50th anniversary by going to the top!"*
> *-9/3/93, Loma Linda, CA*

117

growing number of men and women have done it after a heart attack, amputation, organ transplant, chemotherapy, or other major physical trauma.

We love seeing the multi-generation groups; parents who climb with their children and even grandchildren are creating family memories that will last longer than our tenure.

> *"Aah Hah! I Made it!! And now we're engaged! Yeah!*
> *-5/30/88, Redwood Creek, CA*
>
> *"Married the climb Guide!"*
> *-7/16/88, Sacramento, CA*
>
> *"Honeymoon Trip Stopover Ya Hoo"*
> *-7/10/89, Redwood City, CA*
>
> *"Fell in love here—engaged now"*
> *-9/30/99, Ridgecrest, CA*
>
> *"My b/f proposed to me at Lone Pine Lake"*
> *"She said yes"*
> *-8/1/99, Palmdale, CA*

Wedding anniversaries are often celebrated here too, and vows renewed for the future. One woman climbed the Trail in her original wedding dress, accompanied by her husband of 50 years! Some people meet their "significant other" on the Mountain, and others have come here on their honeymoon.

If you are looking for an exciting way to "pop the question," you might consider proposing on the summit—this will be a story you can tell your grandchildren about, while you climb the trail with them 50 years from now.

Mark Brunke and Gilda Garcia actually got married on the summit. Their wedding took place in July of 1995. This was a very late year for snow, and the wedding party struggled

Summit wedding, July, 1995: Pascal David, Kimiko Kelly, Lorraine Rodriguez, Mercy Powell, Gilda Garcia (the bride in her leopard veil), Mark Brunke (the groom), Shante Jackson-Sposato, Frankie Blue, Karry O'Brien

"Just Married" honeymooners Gilda and Mark on the Trail (photos courtesy of Gilda Garcia & Mark Brunke)

> "Mt. Whitney kept us together"
> -8/2/96, Visalia, CA

valiantly to reach the top. At one point the wind even blew the bride over; makeup and hairdos were forgotten. Everyone was exhausted, but they made it to the summit, as shown in the photos (previous page). Gilda writes,

"Too bad it was so cold because I had a great leopard outfit on under all those clothes. [Above us] are silk 'Tibetan' prayer flags with well-wishes from our friends and loved ones who accompanied us in spirit

> "Lots of work, worth it (beating cancer was easier!)"
> -9/21/00, (not Boston), MA

only. On long expeditions on Mt. Everest, traditionally the flags would be shredded by winds, carrying the messages far."

Other special occasions that people have climbed Whitney to celebrate include triumphs over bad habits such as drugs, alcohol, or smoking; escapes

> "After this, I can do anything"
> -17-yr old probationer,
> Santa Ana, CA

from bad relationships (by both men and women); career changes; moves into or out of California; and of course retirement.

There are some life-changing events that aren't always planned but just happen when people make this climb. Couples who were heading for divorce find they can communicate better without all the

> "My most significant physical feat in my life"
> -6/23/99

120

distractions of home, and their marriages turn around. People without any purpose for living

> *"Hardest part = leaving!"*
> *-7/4/99, San Diego, CA*

discover the forgotten beauty of a bird, a flower, or the sunrise, and find that life is good after all.

Through the efforts of youth organizations such as Boy Scouts of America, and "Beyond Limits," (a community program that takes groups of high-risk youth up Mt. Whitney every year) young people's lives are influenced in a positive way. Kids who were gang

> *"Finally made it after 2 years!"*
> *-Walnut Creek, CA*

members in the city find a new way of life they never could have imagined, and determine to make meaningful changes in their behavior.

We have known people who planned to climb Whitney for one of these occasions but didn't realize they needed permits. Frustrated, they

> *"I could see for miles & miles"*
> *-9/4/91, Manhattan Beach, CA*

celebrate anyway at the Portal, and vow to return with a permit to climb another time. These promises are often kept.

Unfortunately, some people come to Mt. Whitney to end their lives. A few suicides have occurred during our years here. It is sad indeed to think that even these beautiful surroundings could not give a person hope for something better in this life.

> *"Great time, my last Big Adventure as a Scout"*
> *-Troop 670, 8/23/91, Cypress, CA*

121

View from the Road: L-R, Lone Pine Peak, Candlelight, Thor's Peak, "Little Whitney" Needles

Between Lone Pine Peak and Candlelight, Meysan Lakes drainage is easily visible from the Road

IV. BACKGROUND INFORMATION

A. OTHER APPROACHES & LOCAL TRAILS

For anyone planning technical climbs in the Eastern Sierra, we recommend Peter Croft's book, <u>The Good, The Great, and the Awesome</u>. It includes descriptions of Lone Pine

> *"Climbed east face what a rush!"*
> *-6/30/93, Garden Grove, CA*

Peak, Keeler Needle, and many others.

1. <u>East Buttress/East Face</u>

Only experienced climbers should attempt these routes. Both are currently ranked 5.4-5.7. As with any approach to the summit, altitude and unpredictable weather are variables to be contended with. Your approach is via the Mountaineer's Route, up the North Fork drainage of Lone Pine Creek. This brings you to Iceberg Lake, elevation 12,500' (also known as Eastface Lake). From here, both routes ascend the "first tower," from which the East

> *"Up East Buttress, Down Mt. Route, Tired & Hungry"*
> *-5/27/00, Corvallis, OR*

Face route forks to the left, and the East Buttress route heads toward the right. Rockfall is a danger on both of these routes, as well as falling debris from visitors at the summit. Helmets are advised.

2. John Muir Trail

      Mt. Whitney marks the southern end of this 212-mile trail, named after the famous mountain man who helped form the Sierra Club in 1892. The northern end of the "JMT" is in Yosemite National Park. It winds through three national parks, one national monument, and four wilderness areas, following the Sierra crest and passing a number of peaks over 14,000 feet in elevation. We meet hikers who have spent several weeks traversing the entire Trail. More often, people hike short segments. A popular route (but one that covers the most difficult part of the Trail) is to enter the wilderness from the Onion Valley trailhead west of Independence, joining the JMT near Kearsarge

> *"I made it! John Muir Trail yeah!"*
> *-7/30/93, Dortmund, Germany*

Pass. Coming south, the ascent is gentler than the Whitney Trail approach. The JMT turns east for the final climb to the summit of Whitney. A quick descent eastward on the Mt. Whitney Trail ends at Whitney Portal.

      People thinking of starting the JMT after the middle of August from the south end and crossing over Trail Crest into the back country can be caught by snow. Heading north to Yosemite, conditions can get colder with more snow along the way. Also, in some years the back country Rangers start coming out in mid September and the summer resorts start closing due to early snows.

3. Cottonwood Lakes Trail

      For a compromise between climbing Mt. Whitney on a weekend, and taking a month or a whole summer to traverse one of the longer trails, this route makes for a meaningful four-to-seven-day wilderness trek. From Lone Pine, drive up Whitney Portal Road approximately three miles to Horseshoe

Meadows Road. Turn left, and gear down for the steep drive up to the Cottonwood Pass Trailhead. From this starting point there are several ways to reach Mt. Whitney, giving you about 25 miles of hiking at higher elevations in order to acclimatize for the final push to the summit. All of these trails lead to beautiful Lower Crabtree Meadow. After a refreshing stay there, turn toward the east, following the JMT past Timberline Lake, Guitar Lake, and up the west side of Whitney. You know the way from here. Go to the summit and then complete the loop by descending the Whitney Trail to the Portal.

4. Pacific Crest Trail

The Pacific Crest Trail (PCT) is one of eight National Scenic Trails. It runs from the Mexican Border near Campo, California, through Oregon and Washington to Manning Park, Canada, a distance of

> *"Done w/resupplying after 130 miles on the PCT—now onto Tuolumne Meadows—then Sonora Pass."*
> *-7/7/91, Providence, RI*

2,638 miles (4,247 kilometers). The trail follows the "Pacific Crest" along the Sierra Nevada, Cascade, and other mountain ranges. The PCT was created by an act of Congress in 1968, and officially completed in 1993. Approximately 100 people set off from Campo each spring with a goal to reach Canada by fall. Twenty to thirty of them complete the "through-hike." Most PCT visitors enjoy a portion of the Trail at a time. One of the intersections along this route is the JMT spur leading up to Mt. Whitney. PCT hikers may take the side trip down to Whitney Portal, going into Lone Pine for supplies. The John Muir Trail is a popular segment of the PCT. For those who want a longer piece but aren't ready for the whole thing, you can begin at Lake Tahoe and hike the 500 miles south to Mt. Whitney.

5. Other Local Hikes

Adventurous folks who wish to try something besides the "beaten path" of the Whitney Trail may find several other hikes in the area of varying difficulty:

Mt. Muir. Along the ridge above Trail Camp, this peak offers experienced climbers a quick side trip that will add another 14,000-plus summit (14,015, to be precise) to their itinerary. It is not a marked trail; do not attempt to climb it if you are a beginner. It is exposed class 3; some say class 4.

Lone Pine Campground to Whitney Portal National Recreation Trail (NRT). A lovely little hike can be found on the south side of Lone Pine Creek by crossing the bridge next to

> *"Nice but long hike from L.P. Camp"*
> *-7/24/99, California City, CA*

the rest rooms at the Portal and turning left. This upper portion of the NRT offers quiet fishing spots as well as house-sized boulders to clamber up, down, and around. In a few minutes, it takes you down to the Whitney Portal Campground. The entire trail is an easy downhill stroll if you begin at Whitney Portal. From the other direction, it is a bit more strenuous, and should be undertaken early in the morning before the heat of the day. Though only a few miles long, this route covers terrain that varies from a flat desert with sagebrush to a cool forest with towering pines and running water.

Meysan Lakes Trail. The jewel of the Portal area, this trail starts with parking on the Portal Road at the family campground. Unlike the Whitney trailhead, parking is fairly open. From the parking area, go through the campground and cross the bridge toward the cabins. You should see a sign for Meysan Lakes Trail. Follow the trail up through the cabin neighborhood. As it winds somewhat southeast, the trail goes into a canyon where it follows Meysan Creek along the west side. Water is not readily available, and the sun will be on you for most of the trail. Bring plenty of water for the hike up, and refill at the Lakes for your descent.

The Meysan Lakes Trail was rebuilt in the 1994 season, and is fairly easy to follow. For the first few miles, a very sandy slope must be crossed and the trail can be lost in this area. Just keep to the westerly side of the canyon, off the walls, and continue up to the end of the canyon proper. Several false meadows will be crossed. The final meadow will have a granite ledge system about in the middle of the meadow with a small waterfall running most of the time. Head for the waterfall and you will find the trail up and over this last ledge

> *"Meysan Lake"*
> *-10/1/00, Santa Monica, CA*

system. It exits on the bank of Meysan Lake, where you will enjoy great fishing and solitude—a rare find in this part of the Sierras. The hike is about as difficult as climbing the Whitney Trail, so plan a whole day. It's a steep route, traveling 4.7 miles, with nearly 4,000' gain in elevation (from 7,900' to 11,600'). It's ideal if you are staying in the campground and want a very private walk with much scenery. We have found this a great place to hide when Sunday rolls around and we need a "recharge." This canyon also leads you to Lone Pine Peak routes, along with passage to Mt. Irvine and Mt. Mallory. These are not trails, and require mountaineering experience.

6. Backcountry Exploring. Many cross country treks can be reached from the Portal area: Arc Pass, Whitney Pass,

Crabtree Pass, Vacation Pass, Tulainyo Lake, Wallace Lake, Sky Blue Lake, and on into the back country. We get calls all the time for details on "can this [route] be done?" Most of the time Doug Jr. or Sr. have done the trip, in the Whitney backyard. HOWEVER—this doesn't mean you should "get a poke and a pickle" and off you go.

> "On Sat. & Sun. 7 peaks, 4 needles, 1 pinnacle"
> -7/23/93, Portola Valley, CA

We have found many times that what looks like a good canyon or chute on the west side of the range will turn into vertical terrain at the top, or vertical on the east face. A review of the early literature mentions great disappointments as these first ascents were attempted.

We want to emphasize that any cross country travel is not hiking. It will always require technical climbing skills and advanced map reading skills. What looks good on the map will almost always turn into steeper terrain than you expect. We go very light, bringing only a day pack and climbing gear, and have had to travel most of the night on several trips to stay warm and get home with our tails between our legs. Depending on the time of year, storms can make passing from the west side to the east side very dangerous. Several feet of snow can fall in a short time, covering the trails out over the pass at Trail Crest.

> "Tulainyo Lake...starkly beautiful at 12,802 a.b.s."
> -3/1/02, Claremont, CA

Indian Encampment on the Carillon Mesas
by
Marcyn Del Clements

Now the night wind
wakes in the foxtail pines,
and they begin to sing
as a Sturgeon Moon
rises in the south,
rises straight up Lone Pine Peak.

I didn't seek out this solitude
but here I am,
alone on an alpine fell field.

I talk to myself. I talk to my stove.
Every time it fires up on the first match,
I praise it. *You sweet thing*, I say to it.
I talk to the marmot—
he pretends to be stone.
I talk to the ants that
carry off my fallen crumbs.

If I said I talk to God,
it wouldn't be a lie.
Up here—there's just the fox pines,
the meadow flowers
and the turning stars.

—*Previously appeared in "Newsnet," St. Ambrose Episcopal Church Monthly Newsletter, December 2001, ed. by The Rev. Canon Douglas Edwards, Rector*

Whitney Summit via Mountaineer's Route, 7-28-94.
L-R: Dick Hughes, William Ross, Rick Erickson, Bob Stenson, Doug Thompson
(photo courtesy of Rick Erickson)

••••••••••••••••••••••••••

B. MOUNTAINEERS ROUTE

The Mountaineer's Route is an alternate way to the summit that can be climbed without special equipment by experienced mountaineers. John Muir was the first to find this way up, which is a shorter, more direct route than the Trail, but is also steeper and more challenging.

We have decided to include a Guide for the Mountaineer's Route in this second edition, with a caveat to those who are not ready for it: **If an inexperienced hiker attempts the Mountaineer's Route, they are setting themselves up for failure.**

<u>Why You Shouldn't Go If You Aren't Ready:</u>

It has been our observation that inexperienced hikers who try to climb the Mountaineer's Route start up and get stuck. They thrash around in the drainage, trying to find their way, and do a lot of damage to the area. This results in heavy impact on the local wilderness resources. The water, plants, soil, and animals exist in a delicate balance which is easily upset.

This beautiful canyon, in its purest, undisturbed natural form, could yield a truer "Mt. Whitney Experience" than the heavily-traveled Trail, for those who have the skills to enjoy it. It is unfortunate that it has been treated with disrespect by some, and is no longer a pristine area. As John Muir said, this Route is for those with "well-seasoned limbs." His term for the main Trail was the "mule way."

Here are some suggestions for those who are interested in this version of the Whitney Experience and feel they are ready:

- Be aware that this is not a designated trail. It is an established climber's path leading up the North Fork drainage of Lone Pine Creek.

- Just because permits are sometimes available for this route, don't assume that "just anyone" should attempt it. If you aren't able to get a permit for the Whitney Trail, do not use this as a rationale for obtaining a permit for the Mountaineer's Route.

- If you are not an experienced mountaineer with map-reading skills, or able to follow a "climbers trail," don't try it. This Route requires full mountaineering skills.

- If you feel you are ready to try it, consider hiring a guide for your first trip up. We have names of professionals who will help you succeed. The Forest Service Supervisors Office in Bishop is another good source for names of qualified guides.

- If you cannot afford a guide, put up a sign on the bulletin board at your local sporting goods store asking for a climbing partner who knows the Route. You can also post a request on the Internet.

- There are other published Guides available for the Mountaineer's Route. While we realize the authors' intent is good, and they know the Route themselves, it can be deceptive to lead a person up this canyon who is not capable of climbing it.

- Many sources imply some type of easy ingress to the area by a few simple photos. After numerous excursions up this canyon, we have concluded that the most deceptive part of this Route is its severity.

- An experienced mountaineer will do just as well or better with a topo map than with written instructions and photos which can easily be misinterpreted.

Description:

This route, although only 3.4 miles one way, rises 6,000 feet above the Portal, at some points is a class three climb, and IS NOT FOR THE FAINT OF HEART! Again, this is NOT a trail. The route should be easy to follow for experienced climbers. If all of us would use the same path, it would stop the severe damage being perpetrated in this

> *"This mountain is high"*
> *-8/15/99, Poland*

drainage by tramping around on false routes. The path you follow has been used for a long time by mountaineers. Stay on the main route that has been plainly marked. We could talk about cairns/ducks, but we know that all schools of thought will never agree as to what's right. Our opinion: if they are wrong take them down, but if they mark critical points, leave them.

Also, as climbers we should set the example of taking out our own trash and human waste. Before you go, pick up a poop bag at the Store or the Ranger Station. On the way out, you can dispose of used bags in the covered can at the main trailhead at the Portal.

Take the main Whitney trail to the North Fork of Lone Pine Creek sign. This is 150 feet before you reach the John Muir Wilderness Boundary sign. If you have any doubt, stay on the main trail to the Wilderness sign and then come back down the trail 150 feet, re-crossing the Creek. Next, turn around so you're facing up the trail, and head up to your RIGHT on the NORTH SIDE of the North Fork Creek. About 200 feet up this path you will see a sign, "Mountaineer's Route."

Follow this path up through the trees and ferns until it flattens out. This will be about a quarter of the way up the canyon. From here you should see the notch/gap below Lower Boy Scout Lake. Continue on about 100 feet and you will cross to the South side of the stream. There will be somewhat of a tunnel through the willows exiting onto a slab (10' rock).

Follow the path up the South side, below the wall and above the stream. As the canyon narrows down and the path joins the slabs, you will re-cross the stream to the North side. This crossing can be very wet and icy. The stream has two threads at this point. Boulder hop across the first stream of water until you reach a mud slope (about 15 feet). If a log is standing there, avoid it and climb up the mud slope. About 20 feet more will take you to the next crossing, where you'll go down and rock-hop again and cross next to or under a waterfall. Avoid the slick log lying in the water.

> *"Get shape (aut baufin)"*
> *-7/20/99, Iceland*

As you leave the water, go to the wall and turn up the canyon. Fifty feet along the base of the wall will take you to a dead end. This is the start of the Ebersbacher Ledges. Look up and to the right, and you will see the "pine tree." Work your way up the crack to the tree. At the tree, look to the east and the ramp is straight ahead. Stay close to the wall and you should see the path. Walk 150' east on this narrow ramp (level). At this point you will step up, gaining about three feet of elevation. Follow this ramp, continuing east for 175 feet, staying next to the wall (away from the drop-off). This will get you to a short section of stair steps about 5 feet up and about 5 feet east.

MAKE A MENTAL NOTE OF THIS POINT. This is the turning point on the way down. If you miss this and continue on the upper ledge, you will need rope and climbing skills to get down.

As you leave the ledge, head straight for the main wall in front of you. At the base of this wall (100') you will find the path. Follow the path at the base of the wall until it exits onto an open area, and you will see the notch/gap below Lower Boy Scout Lake. From here, the path is easy to follow.

At the notch, lose a little elevation to a sign that reads "No wood fires." Cross here to the south side and follow the path through the

> *"Reminds me [of] the Alps"*
> *-7/26/99, Switzerland*

trees to the boulder field. Look along the base of the left scree slope (left or south side of Lower Boy Scout Lake). You will see the track to follow to the west. Also, you'll see two giant rocks near the waterfall. You will begin climbing here. Head to the downhill side of the lower boulder. Stay close to this rock. As you get to the rock you will see the willows. At the very edge of the downhill side of the lower rock is the path. Follow it into the willows about 15' and it will turn north on a slab and down into a small stream. Cross this stream, work up several feet, and cross another thread of water. You will be to the right of the stream.

As you exit this crossing you will be at a slab. Climb onto the slab and follow it to a group of trees (approximately 1500' distance). These slabs will be icy and very slick—if not icy, mossy, so watch your step at all times through this section.

CAUTION: When you get near Clyde Meadow, do not go into the closed bowl of Upper Boy Scout Lake. Make sure you travel in a southerly curve around the ridge. When you get to the trees (Clyde Meadow), look up and left to the gap/saddle and follow slabs to the path that switchbacks up to this saddle. You will find a grand path at this point.

> *"I swam in Iceberg Lake!"*
> *-10/18/99, Manhattan Beach, CA*

Now that you are here at 11,500'+ elevation, let's talk it over. You have never had to use any more than walking skills. You are about halfway up, and your last water spot is Iceberg Lake which is just above you. Turn around, look to the east, and enjoy the view of the North Fork Drainage. Your line of sight should be almost a straight path to the Portal.

Ascend past the small water-seep below Iceberg Lake. Many old climbers used the west end of the water-seep to climb up to Iceberg Lake, but now most people travel past the water (at certain times of the year it may be a wide waterfall) and go up the next draw to the west. This route

> *"Deep breaths"*
> *-5/23/99, Tokyo, Japan*

is much safer and faster with a pack. It takes you to Iceberg Lake.

The Mountaineer's Route takes the gully to the notch at 14,000'. Several ways will get you to the notch. We suggest taking the left chute just south of the main gully. However, this depends on snow or ice conditions and your skill level. If you take the main chute, rockfall and people in the chute above make it worth staying to the right or left as much as you can. Also, in the middle of the main chute there is a large boulder blocking the path. Don't climb up to it and try climbing around it. Pick a course around it about 50' below and it's fairly easy. The chute above this point is about 45 degrees, and below is about 40 degrees.

From the notch, several choices exist. The traditional Mountaineers Route follows the first chute to the south. Another choice, the "easy walk off," is never easy. It's exceptionally risky if there's snow and ice on this traverse. This is a 50+ degree slope for about a

> *"Mountaineers Route - Yowza!"*
> *-10/19/99, Danville, CA*

quarter mile. Full climbing gear with ice skills and tools are needed. On the other hand, if studied, the first chute to the south of the notch will reveal a path up on rock for most of the summer. Again, this will require climbing skills, and a lot of people turn back at the notch.

The last several hundred feet is not that important. The exposure picks up in this section and is a factor to consider on the way down if you continue up. Some people choose to walk down the main trail after summiting, making it a circle trip. PLEASE NOTE: Taking the Whitney Trail down requires a Whitney Zone Permit. No excuses are accepted, and you will be fined ($200 at this writing) if you don't have the correct permit.

> *"Let's leave K2 & Everest to the elite*
> *And keep The Whitneys for us meek"*
> *-10/6/99, Tasmania/Australia*

Thoughts from Doug Sr.:

One day I was talking to a guy about the Mountaineer's Route and how it has a tendency to attract hikers who have been up the Trail several times, and for something different they want to go up the Mountaineer's Route. Or, the really skilled mathematicians who deduct that this route is only 3.4 miles (versus 11 miles) decide to try it. Others notice that if one goes this way, they do not need a permit for day hikes, and there are guide books for sale that describe the area "to a fashion." These writeups don't include much detail, not wanting to cheat you out of the "discovery" experience that most mountaineers enjoy and expect. But then again, most mountaineers would not buy a book or trust these flowery dream walk descriptions.

Now to the point—as we were chatting, a young woman came to the counter with four tootsie roll pops and three candy bars, and said that last year she and her friend went up Langley and the next hike planned was Whitney. She needed to get home, so her friend did the Mountaineer's Route by himself and took a fatal fall on the "easy walk off" section.

Most people who write these descriptions have very little chance to see how critical good information is. What may have looked good in a drought year can turn into a sheet of blue ice for the next several seasons, and at this Whitney place, skill levels sometimes are a little short of the ego. Climbers at times show bad judgement on the way down the Mountaineer's Route. One day I was going up the last section and noticed two climbers coming down into an ice flow, and I asked if they had a new way down. One admitted they had just soloed the East Face and were clueless as to how to get down. This didn't stop them from starting down with no idea where to go. We have a term for this now, EEA (Ego Exceeds Ability).

Another aspect of this North Fork route is that each storm can change the condition and characteristics. What may be ice and snow one week can turn to waist deep snow that takes hours to travel a mile in. Iceberg Lake can stay frozen until mid-July, and certain parts of the chute will remain snow covered year round.

View of Mountaineers Route
(photo courtesy of William Ross)

Snow-covered Mount Whitney
(photo by William Ross)

●●●●●●●●●●●●●●●●●●●●●●●●●●●●

C. THE MOUNTAIN

Mt. Whitney is the highest peak in the continental U.S., and is located in the Sierra Nevada Mountain Range in California. At an elevation of 14,497.61 feet, it is not a summit to be taken lightly. If you have traveled through Owens Valley on Highway 395, you have passed through its shadow. You may not have noticed its majestic presence. A shy mountain, Whitney rises west of the highway, camouflaged among other mountains of similar size and shape. It is not visible from any other main road.

> *"The mountains are wonderful"*
> *-8/9/88, Vienna, Austria*

You can get a closer look at the mountain by turning west off 395 at the only stoplight in Lone Pine, and heading up to Whitney Portal. If you drive up in the winter, you'll be stopped by snow before you reach the parking lot. But, if you come in the summer, by driving only 13 miles off the interstate's "beaten path," you'll discover a hidden canyon full of beauty, adventure, and a wide variety of interesting people with stories to tell. This microcosm is the closest you can get to Mt. Whitney by car. There are two options for getting closer: a day hike or backpacking (see first section for more information).

Horses and pack animals are used in parts of the High Sierra back country, but are no longer allowed on the Whitney

Trail. The story is told of one such animal who suffered an untimely death on the Trail some years ago. The packers had no time or inclination to properly dispose of it, so they rolled it a short distance off the trail. As days went by, complaints filtered down to the Forest Service regarding a moldering carcass on the Mountain. They got upset and ordered the store owners, who owned a pack outfit at the time, to get rid of the thing. "Don't worry, we'll take care of it," was the reply. And so they did—their dynamite blasts removed all traces of the remains! A similar incident was reported in 1996 on the back side of Whitney.

When you get to Whitney Portal, tilt your head back and look up. This should keep you occupied for a few minutes, and reward your decision to explore. Depending on the weather and the time of day, you may see the sun, the moon, stars, clouds, falling snow, satellites, fighter jets, or experimental aircraft overhead. Mt. Whitney is still hiding in the distance, but its neighboring peaks and ridges already surround you. The hypnotic spell of steeply cliffed granite beckons you to come higher. Most people who visit Whitney Portal for the first time make a vow to come back. As the Guest Book testifies, many of them return, one, two, or twenty-five years later. This is a mountain that leaves a lasting impression.

> *"From now on I can look at Whitney and know!"*
> -8/4/93, Calabasas, CA

> *"Such Granite!"*
> -5/15/88, Chatsworth, CA

> *"BEAUTIFUL!!!"*
> -5/4/99, Antwerp, Belgium

Elevation of Mt. Whitney

Each season we have numerous reports on the elevation of Mt. Whitney. Various maps, books, gift items, and common knowledge range anywhere from 14,493 ft. to 14,501 ft.

To establish the elevation of a point or place, certain things have to happen:

1. There needs to be a base datum.
2. Different methods or procedures can produce varied results.
3. Adjustments of the data are returned corrected for known errors.
4. Results are published based on final adjustments.

Benchmarks are classed by order of procedure to establish predicted results. Some common maps show v.a.b.m. This stands for vertical angle, meaning trig methods

> *"14,495 feet"*
> *-6/16/88, Carson City, NV*

were used to establish elevation. This is not a bad way to establish rough elevation, within one to three feet, but cannot be considered for adjustment into a network because of large probable error.

Another method for establishing rapid elevations is to use an aneroid barometer based on local datum, usually adjusted to local airport barometer. Again, results are reported to the nearest foot. In the past, this was acceptable for the most common use of the findings, which was map making for base maps.

Precise levels can only be reached by measuring the difference of elevation forward and return to the same point. This method provides a check on each benchmark established.

143

Since the only factor is difference of elevation, the base datum can be adjusted and all benchmarks can then be corrected. Now—what about movement between benchmarks? This is very real in California, and states that have crustal motion and sudden movement. Real elevations only exist for the instant they are recorded. Some areas are very stable, others are not.

The published elevation by the U.S. Coast and Geodetic Survey based upon the sea level datum of 1929 reports the first order elevation of b.m. 14,501 ft. This was adjusted in 1940 to 14,494.164 ft. Vertical control, as well as horizontal control, for the United States is now maintained by NOAA (National Ocean and Atmospheric Administration). To get an elevation for a benchmark, contact:

NOAA N/CG 17
SSMC3 Station 09202
Silver Springs, MD 20910
Phone: 301-713-3242

NOAA has readjusted the base datum for the United States. We contacted their office and established if California was to be reported, what would be the correction for Mt. Whitney. It was determined by NOAA that the run through Owens Valley would show a +3.45 ft. to the known elevations. Therefore, a correction to the published elevation of Whitney would be 14,494.164 + 3.45, establishing an elevation of 14,497.614 ft.

We hope this clears up any concern about the elevation of Mt. Whitney. The disks on the summit report several different elevations. Think of these elevations as names for the point and contact NOAA for the current true elevation.

• •

D. THE PORTAL

A few years ago, one campground host responsible for emptying trash and cleaning fire rings used to shovel all refuse, including hot coals, into the back of his pickup truck. By putting slats around the bed of the truck, he increased its capacity and decreased his number of trips down the hill. On more than one

> *"Rarefied"*
> *-8/15/88, Vermont*

trip down the narrow, winding road to Lone Pine, smoke billowed from the heap. While the people at the Portal were aware of the problem, it took several trips before the poor fellow realized he was driving a truckload of fire down the hill to the dump.

There are three campgrounds, a fishing pond, a picnic area, two trailheads, and a cluster of summer cabins in the Whitney Portal area. The Meysan Lakes Trailhead is on the left of the road about 1.5 miles before the end. Just past this trailhead is the Whitney Campground, which contains 44 sites for car camping, four rest rooms, and some great fishing spots along Lone Pine Creek. Immediately west, at the next turnoff, is a small campground with three campsites for larger groups, such as scout troops, family reunions, etc. Farther south, across the Creek, are some private cabins, perched on a

> *"2nd time in 23 years"*
> *-6/28/89, Phoenix, AZ*

145

slope above the campgrounds. The next turnout on the left is the overflow parking lot, designated for backpackers. More parking spaces can be seen along the left side of the road.

> "This pack weighs a ton!"
> -8/30/88, Long Beach, CA

Bulletin boards with information about bears, weather, Forest Service Regulations, and messages to/from hikers mark the Whitney Trailhead on the right. This is the "jumping-off spot" where people launch their Mt. Whitney climbs. Likewise, returning hikers end their treks here, wearily casting off backpacks and boots as they celebrate their accomplishments with sighs of relief. Many hikers actually forget items that they take off when their hike is finished, leaving them at the trailhead area (boots, packs, jackets, etc.).

One day a backpacker came into the store and asked directions to the trailhead. He was told to go back down the road about 20 steps, where it would be easily visible. A few minutes later he returned for more information—he hadn't been able to find it. Once again he was directed toward the trail. When he returned for the third time, the storekeeper firmly advised him that he should reconsider his plan of hiking the mountain. If he couldn't find the beginning of the trail, he was a pretty high risk for getting lost on the way to the summit.

> "Es el mejor lugar de USA
> [It's the best place in the USA]"
> -8/20/99, Long Beach, CA

A little farther along the road, one sees the miniature fishing pond on the left, and a rustic store on the right. The picnic area is found as the road curves left around the west and south edges of the pond, where day parking is available. Two latrines are located on the south side of the pond. Near the junction of the road loop lies a small campground designated for backpackers only. These 10 sites are nothing more than tent pads designed to provide a one-night-only sleeping spot for hikers passing through.

One attraction here that often goes unnoticed is the beautiful waterfall cascading down the southwestern cliffs of the Portal.

> *"I climbed to the top of the waterfall!!!"*
> *-8/22/92, Venice, CA*

We estimate the lower falls at approximately 300 feet. Combined with the upper falls, this Lone Pine Creek runoff tumbles a total of 500-600 feet, making it one of the tallest falls in the eastern Sierra. Earlene especially loves the little resting spot at its base, where she finds refuge from the store crowds. One season a group of drummers performed at the top of the lower falls, sending their rhythms echoing off the rock walls throughout the area.

The waterfall grows and shrinks during various stages of runoff. In the cold weather it quiets down, freezing into beautifully shaped icicles. Although its constant rush is a soothing sound, the increased noise of heavy meltoff sometimes keeps folks awake at night. The falls can usually be seen from the road—a shining white ribbon.

A few words about the pond: it is stocked approximately once a week during the season by the Department of Fish and Game. They vary the days so fishermen won't plan their trips

> *"This place is The Bomb"*
> *-7/18/99, Lexington, KY*

Lower Part of Portal Waterfall (photo by Dave Morrison)

around its arrival. If you can't catch a fish in this pond, you need to quit fishing. Licenses are required for all those over 16. The Whitney Store does not sell fishing licenses; you can buy them in Lone Pine.

A recent improvement to the pond is a wooden platform where wheelchair-bound visitors can cast their lines comfortably. Unfortunately, some folks are rather possessive about their fishing spots. Contrary to what people may tell you, there are no special privileges granted to those who have fished the pond before.

> *"Great Fishin!"*
> *-7/27/89, Downey, CA*

One hot afternoon, an avid fly fisherman threw a cast out into the pond and immediately felt a bite. He began to reel it in, when he heard a loud outburst of Spanish expletives from a woman who was fishing across the pond. At once he realized he had snagged her entire catch, a stringer with five trout languishing in the shallows. After he pulled it in, he returned it to the woman, and they had a good laugh.

> *"Caught my first fish"*
> *-9/8/90, Santa Clarita, CA*

View of the Whitney Store

E. THE STORE

The Store's original cabin structure of 480 square feet was built in 1935. Bruce and Grace Morgan operated the business for over 20 years (from the 1940's to the 1960's), which included pack trains. The building was used as a living quarters, with the store operating out of the front room. Doug remembers one day when someone came into the back (now the kitchen) of the Store to point out the spot where he was born.

During the 1950's, regular pack train clients included Hollywood director Billy Wilder, who

> *"Thanks for being open"*
> *-5/14/88, San Jose, CA*

enjoyed escorting movie stars on one- and two-week trips into the backcountry. Since the ban on pack animals, the Store has changed hands several times, with various adjustments in product offerings, facilities operations, and management styles. The structure has been remodeled a number of times. After an avalanche destroyed the back of the building in 1969 it was repaired and enlarged. The most recent improvements were made in 1997, giving the store an updated appearance and increasing its size by several hundred square feet.

The way the Thompsons look at it, the Whitney Portal

> *"Perfect & fine service!!!"*
> *-5/13/93, Chomutov, Czech Republic*

> *"Nice feast after the mountain"*
> *-6/1/90, Enumclew, WA*

Store has a mission: to serve the people who come in. They sell lip balm, bumper stickers, and sandwiches, but this place is different than a typical convenience store. The range of clientele covers all socio-economic levels, and literally reaches around the world. Serious climbers sample protein bars and electrolyte-replacement drinks. Car campers shop for matches and marshmallows. Backpackers purchase wool socks and water purifying tablets. Cabin people buy postcards. Day hikers and tourists scoop up T-shirts and refrigerator magnets. Unshaven folks coming out of the wilderness hungrily order a hamburger with real fries, a soda or beer, and a shower.

> *"That Shower was Heaven after 9 days in back country!"*
> *-7/23/88, Palmdale, CA*

Aside from the wide variety of products and services the Store offers for sale, there is another commodity exchanged: human contact. People need to be alone sometimes, and that is often the reason they come to wilderness spots. But the need for someone to talk to and share mountain experiences pulls them back to this non-threatening mid-point between civilization and the woods. The Whitney Store is a great place to "hang out." Tables and chairs on the patio invite visitors to stop and chat with each other. The indoor stools were removed after one customer "hung out" for six hours, however. One of the few rules at the store: be considerate of your fellow customers—take turns!

> *"Nice people/good conversation"*
> *-7/20/88, West Germany*

Another attribute of the Store

152

that you may not find at your local junk-food mart: willingness to help in an emergency. Danger is very real on this mountain, and many customers have come in needing help. The Store has functioned as an emergency shelter, a hospital, and a rescue station. This service was not in the original plans of the owners, but when crises happen, they rise to the challenge. Of course there are many needs they cannot meet, but when they can help, they do.

> *"Thank you for the shelter"*
> *-6/20/88, Rotterdam, Holland*

One spring day, a bus coming up the road to the Portal broke down. The 18 Rumanians on board walked the last couple of miles in a freezing snow and sought shelter in the Store. None of them spoke English, but it wasn't difficult to tell what they needed—hot drinks! The front part of the Store is hardly larger than an elevator, but all were invited inside where they purchased coffee, tea, and soup while drying and warming themselves.

> *"The best country store ever"*
> *-7/8/99, Huntsville, AL*

When it started to hail, the crowd was augmented by several campers who came up to get protection from the pounding stones. Somehow room was made for them too, and for three hours the Store looked like one big party with over 30 guests. The hail ended; a replacement bus arrived; the Rumanians were bussed down the hill; and the campers went back to their tents. Such is life at the Whitney Store.

> *"All of 'Mountain Man Doug' & Doug Jr's advice & assistance helped us have a <u>perfect</u> climb. Thanks!"*
> *-7/3/99, TX*

Father Crowley's retreat house (aka. G. P. Putnam house), ca. 1937. This cabin has since burned and been rebuilt (photo courtesy of Eric Jessen).

• •

F. THE CABINS

Another unique and interesting facet of the Whitney Portal area is the lovely tract of summer homes nestled on the south side of Lone Pine Creek. This little community was established as a result of a nation-wide program authorized by Congress in 1915. The National Forest Service, which was sparsely staffed even then, issued special use permits to private citizens allowing them to build. Along with this privilege came a shared responsibility for care and management of the area.

"Through the great living-room window rise the delicate and miraculous granite spires of Mt. Whitney, painted a new color every hour by the winter sun."
-Tom Treanor, LA Times

Building the Whitney Portal Road in 1934 opened up the area for many improvements. Construction of public campgrounds, picnic areas, the Whitney Store, and the summer cabins all took place within the following two decades. The most vital element of support for this burgeoning tourist spot was (and still is) a drinking water system that supplies public and private areas throughout the canyon. Cabins owners continue to play an important role in maintaining and operating this system, under the tutelage of Jack Jessen, who has assisted in its maintenance and repair since the early 1950's. The residents' time and talents have also been employed in assisting with rescues, medical and law enforcement emergencies, fire safety, interpretive and visitor information, and ecological management.

Over the years, the Portal cabins have sheltered many notable characters of the twentieth century. Msgr. John Joseph Crowley originally built the uppermost cabin in the tract, which housed a consecrated chapel intended to be the final station of the cross along the road from Death Valley to Mt. Whitney. The rockwork in this house and garden was done by the same Italian stonemasons who built Scotty's Castle in Death Valley.

After the "Desert Padre's" untimely death in 1940, the first Whitney ranger, Chuck Short, lived in this cabin year-round as a guest of subsequent owner G. P. Putnam, Jr., son of the New York publishing scion. Mr. Putnam was married to Amelia Earhart when she disappeared while flying over the South Pacific. He later wrote a book about her, and also authored a volume about Whitney Portal: *Up In Our Country*.

> *"Perched on the steep southern rampart of the Portal a mile below where the canyon dead-ends in rocky walls, our house stands where the worst of the winter tempests habitually end."*
> -G. P. Putnam, *Up In Our Country*, p. 37

One of the current cabin owners is a relative of author/naturalist John Muir, and shares a love of the Sierra with his famous progenitor. The long list of residents and visiting celebrities includes prominent physicians, educators, engineers, authors, publishers, executives, athletes, actresses, inventors, musicians, movie producers, and military leaders.

While tourists and campers should and do respect the privacy of cabin owners, there is a friendly atmosphere among these summer residents. Many are happy to show off their cabins and the nearby trails, pointing out unique features of the structures along with the local flora and fauna. Each cabin is distinctive in design and decor, but many contain rock and timber work constructed by Dean Prewitt, a mountaineer who also restored the Smithsonian Institution's stone shelter on top of Mt. Whitney for the National Park Service.

> *"In loving memory of Rolly McNeill, Cabin 11, Whitney Portal - all of your children love you!"*
> *-6/5/00*

One of the cabins contains timbers originally milled at Mammoth Lakes in 1900 and reclaimed from an old Owens Valley soda bin. Two cabins were originally located at the old town site of Manzanar—they were dismantled, hauled up the Portal Road, and reassembled. One cabin contains a fireplace mantle made of tufa blocks mined from the Mono Tunnel extension of the Owens Valley aqueduct. Another cabin has siding from giant redwood milled in the western Sierra. The cabin with the largest fireplace also boasts a chandelier originally from the Marion Davies mansion on Santa Monica beach. One cabin is uniquely situated atop a large boulder. Two cabins have actually housed grand pianos; one

> *"Simply gorgeous"*
> *-5/29/99, Zambia*

of these also contained a library of over 8,000 books at one time.

Only one of the cabins was designed by an architect. The plans for another came from a book of cabin designs published by *Sunset* magazine in 1942. Three of the original cabins have fallen prey to disasters: two suffered serious damage during the great winter storms of 1969, and one was destroyed by fire in 1950. All three of these have been rebuilt. Some of the cabins have names: "Shangri-la;" "Idlehours;" "Haukelei" (which means "hawk's nest" in Norwegian); and "Mandolay."

Many of the cabins are graced by lovely gardens of native and imported flowers and shrubs. Several boast stories of bear visits, including one gentle beast who carefully entered the kitchen window, consumed the residents' gourmet meal, and quietly exited, leaving only a few scratches on the cabinets as a token of his gratitude. This all took place while the owner and his guests had stepped out for a few minutes to a neighboring cabin to watch for a bear that they heard was in the neighborhood!

A few cabin owners have been residents of neighboring Lone Pine, but most have hailed from more distant California cities including Santa Barbara, Alhambra, Los Angeles, Santa Cruz, and Hollywood. Eight cabins are still owned by the families who originally built them, and a legacy of mountain memories fills each one. The young fathers, mothers, and children who summered in the canyon and climbed Mt. Whitney in the 1950's and 1960's can still be seen in the black and white photos of the era.

Each cabin family shares a special love for this mountain and the surrounding area. Even after they have sold their cabins, many former residents return to the tract for various social events, or just to renew friendships with their Whitney neighbors. A total of 62 families have owned the summer homes, making for many years of recreational residence enjoyment and assistance to the visitors of Whitney Portal and Mt. Whitney.

A family vacation mishap first brought Jack Jessen to Whitney Portal. He has owned two of the cabins and has been involved in maintenance of the cabin water system since the early 1950's.

Welcome to Lone Pine

Lone Pine residents take a break in front of their family business. L-R: Tony, Robin and Rebecca Weatherly; Cassidy, Amanda, and Robert Lane

G. THE COMMUNITY

Visitors passing through Owens Valley are not usually impressed. It is flat and barren, boasting no obvious attractions either natural or man-made. It is hot in the summer and boring in the winter. Most folks hurry along, minds set on their respective destinations, hoping their cars don't break down. There is no evidence that a paradise resembling Shangri-La is almost within walking distance. Even while the hot wind blows through ghost towns below, fish-filled creeks gurgle and sing their way among fragrant Jeffrey Pines beside the outdoor restaurant tables at Whitney Portal up above.

> *"Dopo il deserto la vita [after desert...life!]"*
> *-7/30/93, Milano, Italy*

One of the many paradoxes of Mt. Whitney is its proximity to Los Angeles. If you are one of the millions who live somewhere in the midst of LA County, filled to the brim with the newest hip-hop, stars, and styles, teeming with smog, crime, and graffiti, you can get to this wonderful retreat by simply packing an ice chest, gassing up your car, and taking the nearest freeway on-ramp. Depending on what part of LA you live in, your drive to Mt. Whitney is only four to six hours. Caught up in the lifestyle of the City of Angels, however, many of its residents are not even aware this place exists.

On the other hand, people travel from all over the world to get a first-hand look at this awesome Peak. The Guest Book at the Whitney Store contains hundreds of entries from far-off

> *"I didn't know this was on this planet"*
> *-6/11/93, Long Beach, CA*

lands, as well as the other 49 states. Visitors have come from Australia and New Zealand; England and France; Japan and South Africa; Alaska and Florida; China, Poland, and Russia. Customers have entered comments in many tongues, including Italian, German, Dutch, Norwegian, and Portuguese, as well as widely varying styles of English.

One group of Japanese came to camp one summer, bringing their rice cooker. They hadn't realized there was no electricity available, so they were at a loss for feeding their families. The store owners generously allowed them to plug in the appliance each morning for their daily preparation of rice. In exchange, the store owners were given a healthy portion for their own consumption. One

> *"Fantantio Lugar [fantastic place]"*
> *-9/27/88, Brazil*

couple who regularly visit the Portal met a family of Germans at the trailhead. In broken English, the foreigners asked the Californians about water purification. The couple gladly shared their iodine tablets with their fellow climbers. Such international exchanges are common among visitors at the Portal.

Whitney Portal is part of the community of Lone Pine in Owens Valley. Lone Pine's local literature boasts of Whitney's height, along with the notoriety of the annual Lone Pine Film Festival and the depth of nearby Death Valley. It is a small town with a lot of potential. There are several hotels, gas stations, and restaurants; a post office; a

> *"Great to be out of smog & concrete"*
> *-8/21/88, Northridge, CA*

162

*View of Mt. Whitney (refer to arrows) from
Lone Pine's lone stoplight*

grocery store; and even a video rental store. Mount Whitney T-shirts and postcards can be purchased at several souvenir shops.

To the north, Independence houses the Eastern California Museum, where the history of Owens Valley can be appreciated. To the south, an Inter Agency Visitor Center provides information on the many local attractions, as well as models of landmarks on display and a nice selection of books for sale. This Center is a joint effort built and maintained for the community by eight different government agencies: Bureau of Land Management, California Department of Fish and Game, Inyo County, California Department of Forestry, Toiyabe National Forest,

"Relaxing, mind blowing, terrific"
-6/10/99, Louisiana

Inter Agency Visitor Center, just south of Lone Pine (Mt. Whitney is to the right of the flag)

Mono County, Los Angeles Department of Water and Power, California Department of Transportation, Death Valley National Monument, Sequoia-Kings Canyon National Parks, and Inyo National Forest.

The key word in this community's past is Water. Bitter battles were fought in previous decades regarding the rights of resident ranchers versus thirsty (and wealthy) Los Angeles businesses. The big city won, and an aqueduct slurps up the runoff from the eastern side of the Sierras, keeping Owens Lake dry.

The good news: in retrospect, loss of water rights may have been the biggest factor in preserving this area for us to

> *"I was on my way to Death Valley..."*
> *-8/13/89, Sarasota, FLA*

enjoy. If the ranchers had won, Owens Valley might have become another San Fernando Valley,

> *"The beer made me do it!"*
> *-8/18/89, Houston, TX*

bringing smog and ski lifts to deface the slopes of Mt. Whitney.

The nearby Alabama Hills are another local attraction. Picturesque, gnarled formations can be seen as you drive up Whitney Portal Road just outside of Lone Pine. Along with the majestic Mt. Whitney landscapes, these rocky foothills have served as backdrops for dozens of Hollywood-made movies and international films. These productions

> *"The Rock meets The Rock"*
> *-6/2/99, Houston, TX*

bring in movie crews, and more spending money. As the world continues to shrink, and more people pass through Owens Valley, this community will continue to grow.

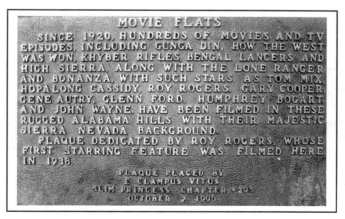

Movie Flats plaque at the intersection of Movie Road and Whitney Portal Road, dedicated by Roy Rogers in 1990 (photo courtesy of Russell Simon)

165

View of Mt. Whitney through eye of Needle in Alabama Hills

*Rattlesnake Mountain, in the Alabama Hills
(photo courtesy of Russell Simon)*

• •

H. A BRIEF HISTORY

1. Native Americans

     The Southern Piute Indians of the Mono tribe were long-time residents of the Owens Valley before the White Man arrived. These families subsisted on pinyon nuts and small animals such as rabbits, birds and lizards. They cooked in expertly crafted baskets, and moved about according to the weather and the food supply. They lived up in the cool canyons during the summers, and retreated to the warmer valley floor during the winters. There is much evidence that they crossed the Sierra range regularly to trade with their distant cousins on the west

> *"Truly spiritual experience"*
> *-6/10/88, Greenbelt, MD*

side. Through several mountain passes, pinyon nuts and red paint were carried to be exchanged for animal skins, acorns and shell beads.

     One archaeological site can still be identified in the Whitney Portal area. On the south side of Lone Pine Creek, several large boulders converge to form a shelter where Indian artifacts rest in the earth and fire markings scar the granite. It has not been proven that Indians ever scaled Mt. Whitney, but a fascinating legend has been handed down that tells how the two needles just to the south of the summit came to be. The current names of these landmarks are Keeler Needle and Day Needle. They have also been called the "Little Whitneys."

167

Piute Legend of the Little Whitneys

A group of animals lived in the mountains. Bear and Coyote were there, among others. Fox was the leader. They hunted every day. When they returned to camp, they dried skins and cooked the meat. They left these things in their camp when they went hunting the next day. When they returned, their things were gone. After this happened several times, they held a meeting to try to find out who had stolen from them. They could not find any tracks, so they decided it was something that came from the sky.

> *"I have Shoshone family here in the Owens Valley. My Roots are here"*
> *-7/10/99, Winslow, AZ*

The following day, they left Hummingbird to watch while they went hunting. He saw a swarm of bees descend to the camp and take all the skins and meat. They flew away to the west, and Hummingbird followed them. After awhile he saw the ocean. The bees flew over a ridge, and Hummingbird knew their home was nearby. He went back to camp and told Fox what he had seen.

In the morning, Hummingbird led all the animals to the place near the ocean. It was a long way. They found the ridge and beyond it they discovered a cave. Bees were flying around the opening. Fox bravely went in to get the things that were stolen. A big bee attacked him with a knife. Fox and all the other animals ran away, and the bee chased them. Finally, he caught up to them and killed all of them except Hawk, who was too fast. The bee chased Hawk around a lake, into the ground,

168

back up into the sky, and all over the world. Hawk became tired, so he decided to make a trap.

When he came to Mt. Whitney, he plucked two of his longest feathers and put them to the south of the mountain. The bee flew between the feathers and was caught. Then Hawk killed him. The two feathers are the Little Whitneys.

Artist's sketch of the Little Whitneys (by Ken Mahoney)

Horace Elder cleaning snow from hooves of "Mattie" on top of Mt. Whitney in a snowstorm. Mules were used in many of the early expeditions (photo courtesy of Eastern California Museum)

• •

2. First Ascents and Place Names

The claim to Whitney's first ascent was hotly debated
for a few years, along with its rightful name. The peak was
actually named Mount Whitney in 1864 when it was discovered
(but not climbed) by a field party of the California Geological
Survey, which included William Brewer and Clarence King.
The men called it the "culminating peak of the Sierra," and
named it after Josiah Whitney, who was a Professor at the
California Academy of Sciences, and founder of the California
Geological Survey (in other words, he was their boss). King
tried twice to climb it on this trip, but was unsuccessful. He
returned in 1871 to try again, and believed he had reached the
summit on this third attempt. So did everyone else, for a time.
This "false Mt. Whitney" that King climbed is at the headwaters
of Tuttle Creek, several miles south of the real Mt. Whitney, and
is now known as Mt. Langley.

The three men who made the first ascent of the "true
Mt. Whitney" were Charley Begole, Johnny Lucas, and Al
Johnson, reaching the proud peak at noon on August 18, 1873.
[August 18 is also Doug Sr.'s birthday. Could this be another
"how did we end up here?"] These residents of Lone Pine
climbed the peak as a diversion, and were dubbed the "Three
Fishermen." It doesn't take much imagination to see the irony
in this story. Poor Mr. King craved the first ascent so badly that
he tried three times, exhausting all of his supplies, to reach the
summit. When he finally thought he had accomplished the feat,
he had actually climbed the wrong mountain. (Because of the
cloudy weather, he was unable to see the higher peak to the

north.) When his error was discovered two years later, he hurried back to California from the East Coast to try once again. He climbed the real Mt. Whitney on September 19, falling into fourth place in the contest. Besides the three fishermen, two other parties reached the summit before King.

> *"Ruggedly High!"*
> *-5/19/88, Bristol, Avon, Great Britain*

Residents of Owens Valley wanted to name the mountain "Fisherman's Peak" to pay homage to the first climbers. They certainly felt closer to these three local friends than to Dr. Whitney. When this was challenged, they proposed the name "Dome of Inyo." Over the next two years, the local newspaper published many articles arguing this issue. Finally a bill which would make "Fisherman's Peak" the official name was introduced in the State Legislature. A strange twist of fate brought the bill before the Senate on April Fools Day, 1881, where they frivolously amended it to read "Fowler's Peak." The Governor ended the silliness by vetoing the bill, and so today the original name stands: Mount Whitney.

John Muir made his first ascent of Whitney on October 21, 1873, just a month after Clarence King finally reached the summit. Muir tried the southwest approach, as all had done before, but ended up dancing all night among the needles to keep from freezing. He returned to Independence where he refreshed himself, and then made his

> *"John Muir had balls!"*
> *-8/9/91, Glenwood Springs, CO*

172

way up the east side, the first to have done so. His course roughly followed what is now known as the "Mountaineer's Route," along the North Fork of Lone Pine Creek.

Other early climbers included a student, a photographer, and in 1878, a group with the first four women to reach the summit. One of these, Miss Anna Mills, is described as being "lame," and may therefore lay claim to the first ascent by a person with a disability.

The first overnight stay at the summit took place on September 2-3, 1881. Captain Otho E. Michaelis, along with two or three other members of an expedition camped on the west side, hauled a tent and a quarter-cord of wood to the top. The wind was so fierce they could not put up the tent, and their campfire burned all the wood long before the sun came up.

> *"...this station...is everything that I could have hoped to find, and more; but existence is only possible on the summit with permanent shelter, for though at the moment I viewed it it was calm, yet the wind and cold would be fatal to life at other times, without house and fire."*
> *-8/24/1881, S. P. Langley*

Like many others since, they did not get any sleep during their night on top of Mt. Whitney. This party, led by Prof. Samuel Langley, consisted of several professors and scientists who were interested in the unique opportunity for scientific observation that this peak offered. Its level area on top, and the abundance of stone for building material, led to the suggestion that a permanent shelter be constructed on the summit.

Mule train on the Mt. Whitney Trail
(photo courtesy of Eastern California Museum)

・・・・・・・・・・・・・・・・・・・・・・・

3. <u>Who Built the Trail, and When?</u>

Gustave F. Marsh
Builder of the Trail and Summit Shelter

Authors' Note: We are extremely grateful to George Marsh, grandson of Gustave F. Marsh, for the material included in this chapter. He has shared generously from his own research, including some never-before-published family photos.

* * *

The original trail from the east side to the summit of Mount Whitney was completed by the community of Lone Pine under the leadership of Gustave F. Marsh on July 18, 1904. Mr. Marsh was also responsible for completion of the summit shelter in 1909 for the Smithsonian Institution. This rock house

Elizabeth & Gustave Marsh (1901)

was used for scientific observations in 1909, 1910, and 1913, and stands today as a notable landmark.

Gustave was born in England in 1869, came to the US in 1890, and became a citizen in 1902. He first became acquainted with mountaineering by working in the mines in Colorado. Other work brought him to Owens Valley where he met and married Elizabeth Dodge in 1901. They settled in Lone Pine, where he took over the local U.S. Mail route, and also carried Wells Fargo Express and passengers. He designed a local water system in 1902, and built southern Inyo County's first telephone line in 1903. He became thoroughly committed to the improvement of Lone Pine and the surrounding area. It was his goal to make Mount Whitney an important asset to the community. Gustave was quick to realize that it could become important to scientists and tourists. Because he was a newcomer in Lone Pine, it took him several years to convince the community to take action.

He worked hard to raise funds and volunteers to build the trail. When the first team ran out of money and motivation, Marsh raised more cash and led a fresh team for a second assault in 1903, finishing the trail in 1904. Charles G. Abbot of the Smithsonian Institution wrote, "Under the leadership of G. F. Marsh the trail was completed to the Summit. Funds were scanty, and it was only by the greatest economy, pluck and perseverance that Mr. Marsh succeeded in getting the trail to the top."

Professor J. E. Church, University of Nevada, persuaded Marsh to accompany him on a winter climb in March of 1905. They spent eight days trying to gain the summit but were turned back by avalanche conditions at approximately 13,500 feet. From a letter Marsh wrote to Church in 1930: "You remember

> *"[It] reflects very high credit on Mr. Marsh and his supporters that the trail was ever completed"*
> *-C. G. Abbot, Smithsonian Institution*

when we went over Whitney Pass and the whole mountain started down, it sure did not feel so good. And then walking in that deep soft snow and to come under that great comb of snow hanging over us. How we tried and shoveled and tried again and how you said we are taking our lives in our hands every five minutes, so I said we had better quit. I wish you could have seen that place when the snow was gone. It would make you shiver."

Gustave's interest in meteorology resulted in contact with Professor Alexander McAdie, Chief of the U.S. Weather Bureau Office in San Francisco. McAdie, who had recommended Mount Whitney for a weather observatory, was

Gustave & son Gus (1905)

notified of the completion of the trail. He subsequently recommended Marsh to Dr. William W. Campbell, Director of the University of California Lick Observatory on Mount Hamilton. (Dr. Campbell later became President of the University of California (UC) System.) A serious plan to build a shelter on the summit began to form.

Gustave accompanied Dr. Campbell and C. G. Abbot, Director of the Smithsonian Astrophysical Observatory, to the summit in 1908, where they decided to construct the shelter. At this time, the trail was in need of repair and improvement to accommodate the transport of materials and instrumentation to the summit. Before the project could be started, Marsh was required to commit that the trail would be in good shape at no expense to the Smithsonian Institution.

Gustave Marsh donated much of his own time on this project and was paid only for the hours spent building the shelter. He worked tirelessly day and night, staying on the summit while others descended to rest or retreat from storms. He is credited with making Mt. Whitney available to science, as

178

for many years the hut was the world's highest astronomical and atmospheric study station.

Abbot recorded, "Marsh worked at all kinds of jobs himself—cooking, breaking stone, carrying stone, carrying snow for water, riveting and cementing, as well as general bossing. He will never get paid in this world for the work he did on that house."

Dr. Campbell reported, "It [the Mount Whitney shelter] is a great credit to the Smithsonian Institution and to the superintendent of the construction, G. F. Marsh, a public-spirited citizen of Lone Pine, who struggled, valiantly and successfully against the difficulties of transporting cement and steel to the summit, as well as difficulties of less open character. Marsh's connection with the project is one in which he is entitled to feel the utmost pride...."

Marsh's own words, in a 1930 letter to Prof. Church:

"To him [Marsh] more than any other one man is due the successful completion of the trail and the building of the observatory"
-A. McAdie, U.S. Weather Bureau

"During the time of putting up the building I stayed on top 43 days. I had 15 men to start with and only 5 at the finish. We had a terrible thunder storm when we were almost done. Our cook was knocked down by a flash of lightning at 9 o'clock one night and another flash almost finished us all. But the storm passed in a few minutes. Leaving all jagged points of rock and squares on the sand screen and the fuzz on the ropes one mass of lights. St. Elmo's Fire, we did not know what it was. So you can guess how scared we was. I urged the men to work fast so as to get done and get away.

Walls going up - Marsh, left of back door

When next day at about 5 P.M. we heard muttering of thunder way over towards Arizona and the clouds rolled up the mountain just as the sun went down. I wish you could have seen those clouds in red suns rays, If Hell was ever turn loose it was in those clouds. I told the men to get under cover and we would be alright. But one by one they ran down the mountain and left me alone. So I went to bed and covered up my head, like a kid, till the storm passed over. I was alone 3 days. Then the men came back and we was glad all around. Prof. Abbot came up a few days after, just as the work was done. I got every thing completed 24 hours ahead of time and $250.00 below my estimate. So I was happy…."

Modern-day visitors may not be impressed by the sight of this humble house. Some assume its parts were flown in by helicopter. A better appreciation for its solidity can be felt when one realizes the task was undertaken without modern conveniences. Water was obtained by melting snow. Wood and cement were hauled up by mules. Stone was broken, shaped, riveted and cemented with hand tools. All this hard labor was performed at an altitude where oxygen is scarce and temperatures vary drastically. Amazingly, the whole project was completed in a little over one month, for about $5,000. (See Appendix B for a feature news article published in 1909, "The Highest House in America")

Several scientific expeditions soon took advantage of the stone hut. In 1909 Dr. Campbell returned with others, bringing a 16" horizontal reflective telescope and a spectroscope. They were able to end a significant controversy by determining that no water vapor existed in the Martian atmosphere.

In May of 1910, Gustave went to the summit of Mount Whitney alone, as no one would go along. He checked to see how the shelter had held

> *"The comet was in plain view as soon as it was dark & just before the moon was covered [by the eclipse] . . . the tail almost reached the moon, it swept almost across the [entire] sky."*
> *-6/5/10, Gustave F. Marsh*

up through the hibernal harshness, and retrieved the temperature data recorded during the past winter.

McAdie wrote, "I received a telegram from Mr. G. F. Marsh, of Lone Pine, saying that he climbed Mount Whitney and reached the summit yesterday (May 23, 1910) and found our instruments left there last August all right. He gives the lowest temperature on the top of the United States proper last winter as 23° F below zero and the highest, 57° F."

Gustave had another reason for summiting on this particular date. It was a unique opportunity to observe Halley's Comet and a total eclipse of the moon, and he did not miss it. He had the best unaided view of both events in, at least, the entire United States. Marsh was up most of the night as he watched the moon darken with the earth's shadow. Suddenly the comet appeared, larger than expected, quite bright, and very beautiful. Eventually it dove into a fog bank to the west,

181

with the tail streaming behind. (See Appendix C for Marsh's own account of this remarkable experience.)

Mr. Marsh repaired the trail in 1913 for a Smithsonian expedition that studied nocturnal radiation from the summit. In 1926, another study took advantage of the conditions on Mt. Whitney to observe the earth's cosmic rays.

Marsh raised his three children in Lone Pine, where he continued to be active in the community. It seems he never wasted any time or material. He served on the school board of trustees for 16 years and as a County Supervisor for one term. He was totally committed to the future of Lone Pine, and he thought it was the most lovely place in the world. He enjoyed the view of Mount Whitney during the day and stars in the clear sky at night for his 46 years there.

Gustave is given credit for two sayings, one from his son Gus: "Nova rich, they blew it before they learned to spend it." And the other from G. P. Putnam: "Englishmen you meet seem to be going home. Americans appear always to be on their way to the office."

Shelter on the summit: Gustave Marsh (left) and Bill Skinner. Photo taken in 1910 by C. G. Abbot (courtesy of George Marsh, grandson of G. F. Marsh)

182

MOUNT MARSH

In 1937, Chester Versteeg named Mount Marsh in honor of Gustave F. Marsh. Versteeg wrote, "G. F. Marsh, of Lone Pine, California. Builder of the first trail to the summit of Mount Whitney from the east in 1904 and the builder of the Smithsonian Institution shelter house on its summit in 1909. The Englishman who fought prejudice, high altitudes, the jagged Sierra Crest, desertion, the elements--but finished the job."

The first ascent of Mount Marsh was done August 25, 1940, by Chester Versteeg, Andy Hennig, Bob Rumohr, and John Wiggenborn. Unfortunately, the record of the peak's name was lost to history for a time.

Mr. George Marsh, grandson of G. F., sustained a persistent effort toward gaining recognition of the name, Mount Marsh. His efforts were recently rewarded. The U.S. Board on Geographic Names (USBGN) made the name Mount Marsh official January 10, 2002.

View of Mount Marsh from Lone Pine Lake
(photo courtesy of George Marsh)

Location: *1.2 miles south-southeast of Mount Whitney and 0.2 miles north-northwest of Mount McAdie*
Elevation: *13,550 feet*

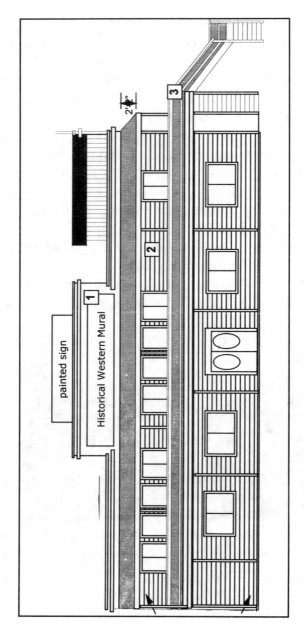

Artist's conceptual drawing of the future Whitney Portal "Town Store" and Lodge to be located in Lone Pine

•••••••••••••••••••••••••

4. <u>Lone Pine and Father Crowley</u>

As more people came to visit Mt. Whitney, more accommodations were built. The original Whitney Portal Road was constructed in 1933-35, making it possible for tourists to drive their automobiles up from Lone Pine into the lush little canyon. Public campgrounds, picnic areas, a store, a tract of summer homes, a pond, and a potable

> *"...,one of the crew that built the pond 1934"*
> *-6/25/88*

water system were all planned and built in the 1930's, making this area more accessible to the general public. The summit shelter was restored during this period by the National Park Service. Cabins were built and rebuilt up through the 1940's and early 50's. The Whitney Portal Road was rebuilt in the 1960's. Other more recent improvements have included the addition of overflow parking lots, and the upgrading of campgrounds. Today's emphasis is not on improving the facilities at Whitney Portal, but on preserving them. Overuse of the fragile Mt. Whitney environment has made it necessary to limit the number of visitors through a quota system of permits.

> *"Climbed Mt. Whitney 1917. 6 in party—horses"*
> *-7/7/89, La Jolla, CA*

The historic Mount Whitney pack trains, originally part of the Portal Store operation, have been eliminated as well. People are welcome here, but must be willing to take their turn—by

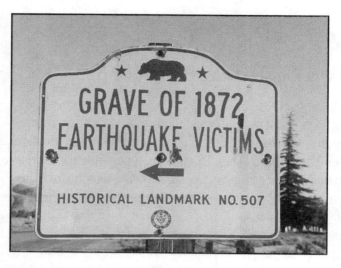

waiting for a trail permit, reserving a camp site, or standing in line at the Whitney Store.

The lifeline to Owens Valley is Highway 395, which runs north and south through this mystical plain between the White/Inyo Mountains and the Sierra Nevada. The mountain ranges rising on either side of the Valley provide the most dramatic scenery to be had in the area. Bishop is the largest city along this route, and lies about 60 miles north of the road to Whitney Portal. Heading south from Bishop, Big Pine is the next dot on the map, followed by Independence, and finally Lone Pine. Each of these little towns has its own personality, and its particular landmarks.

It takes less than five minutes to drive through Lone Pine. There is only one traffic light in the town. Nothing about its appearance belies the colorful history it holds. Even the tree it was named for has disappeared, washed out in a flood.

The first white residents built a shelter on Lone Pine Creek in 1861. More people came to raise crops and live-stock, building homes of adobe. The earthquake of 1872 destroyed most of the buildings, and killed 29 people. Nearby mines soon brought a transient population mixing Mexican, Welsh and Cornish immigrants. The town slowly grew, its patch of green widening as citizens planted orchards and fields of alfalfa.

> *"Dad had pack train out of Hunter's Flat"*
> *-5/18/00, Belfair, WA*

The Carson & Colorado Railroad, running through Owens Valley, was completed in 1883 in hopes of a rich commerce with local silver mines. Among these mines was the Cerro Gordo, atop the Inyos due east of Whitney Portal. This was the southernmost of the famous Comstock Load, from which the Hearst family derived its initial wealth.

The ups and downs of silver prices, along with the inconsistency of the area's mines, took local settlers through economic extremes of prosperity and hard times.

One of those who helped bring new life to the Valley was Msgr. John J. Crowley, a Catholic priest who served in this parish in the 1930's, after serving as Chancellor of the Diocese of Fresno/Monterey. A dedicated and hard-working man, the "Desert

Msgr. John Joseph Crowley saying Mass atop Mt. Whitney (photo courtesy of Eric Jessen)

Padre" began his typical day with a six a.m. mass in Death Valley. Leaving at seven a.m., he drove from below sea level up and down two mountain ranges, arriving in Lone Pine to perform the 9:00 a.m. mass. This ended at 10:00, when he would race north to say mass at 11:00 a.m. in Bishop. Monsignor Crowley became known for the wear and tear he put on his automobiles.

An important goal the Padre worked toward was to unite the people in his parish—not just Catholics, but all men, women, and children—and to instill a sense of pride in the community. The downtrodden residents had become bitter over their past losses, and Father Crowley brought them reasons to smile again. A jovial

> *"Laughter is as important as food and drink and the shirt on your back."*
> *-Msgr. J. J. Crowley*

soul, he organized street carnivals and local plays. He formed the Inyo Associates, a Chamber of Commerce of local editors, miners, farmers, and merchants. Cutting through an atmosphere of mistrust and intrigue, he joked his way into their hearts. He saw a vision for the future of this desert valley in its potential for tourist attractions. He also knew there was a water shortage.

Father Crowley proposed that a dam be built to the north which would ensure adequate water for Owens Valley residents as well as thirsty Los Angeles. He wrote columns about the Valley, lectured about it in Los Angeles, and drew newspaper reporters and photographers with his unusual publicity tactics.

One of these was a special mass at the top of Mt. Whitney, which attracted the attention of people all over the country. Another was a "Fishermen's Mass," said at three a.m. on the morning of the first day of fishing season. The Father invited all fishermen of all religions, along with the media. His little church was packed with Valley friends who happily listened to his three-minute sermon discussing Jesus, the greatest fisherman. The tradition of a "Fishermen's Mass" is still carried on in the Valley today.

Another press event was staged by the Padre to promote a new road joining the lowest point in the U.S. (Death Valley) with the highest (Mt. Whitney). The Wedding of the Waters began as Indian runners filled a gourd with pure, icy water from the nation's highest lake (Lake Tulainyo) just below Mt. Whitney's sum-mit. The gourd was transported in turn by pony express, burro, covered wagon, mule team, railroad car, and airplane. Finally, it

> *"We grant you ownership of the ... water rights. I'm here to fight for human rights."*
> -Msgr. J. J. Crowley

was sprinkled from the airplane into Badwater at Death Valley, the lowest body of water in the U.S. News of the two extreme points involved in this fascinating ceremony spread all over California and beyond. Tourists began to pour into the Valley, bringing dollars and economic growth never before experienced by the sleepy little town of Lone Pine.

The area of Whitney Portal continued to attract more visitors, and a tract was surveyed for 30 cabin sites. Father Crowley began construction of his own mountain home on one of the plots, overlooking Lone Pine Creek and the Valley he loved. Unfortunately, he was killed in an auto accident shortly after the cabin was completed.

Eventually the dreamed-of dam was built north of Owens Valley, and the lake it formed now bears the name of the fondly remembered Father Crowley.

5. Hollywood

In 1920, Lone Pine was changed forever when a silent movie, "The Roundup," was filmed in the Alabama Hills. Since then, over 300 movies, TV episodes, and commercials have been shot on location in the area, immortalizing the striking rock formations and taking advantage of the picture-perfect weather. From "Gunga Din" to "Maverick," from "The Lone Ranger" to "Tremors," movie stars, sets, cameras, and equipment have rolled in and out of town. Many movies were partially filmed at Whitney Portal, including "High Sierra," "The Long, Long Trailer," and "Star Trek 7." The list of visitors is long and impressive: Hopalong Cassidy, Roy Rogers, Humphrey Bogart, Susan Hayward, Spencer Tracy, Ida Lupino, Natalie Wood, Clint Eastwood, Kirk Douglas, John Wayne, Steve McQueen, Shelly Winters, Luci and Desi Arnaz, Willie Nelson, Mel Gibson, and many others. Elephants, horses, and jeeps have all thundered across the rugged backdrops of rock and sky.

Lone Pine facilities provide food and shelter for the visiting celebrities, and residents love to share their experiences as movie "extras." Film crews' visits are unpredictable and irregular, but their comings and goings do boost the town's economy. The annual Lone Pine Film Festival in October also fills local motels and restaurants with movie buffs who enjoy reliving some of the silver screen's greatest scenes.

When the Whitney Store operated the Mount Whitney Pack Trains, in the 1940's and 1950's, movie people including Billy Wilder (Director), William Wilder (Producer), and Elizabeth Taylor were taken from the Portal into the back country as far as Tuolumne Meadows in Yosemite National Park.

Nowadays, most Hollywood types do not venture beyond the Alabamas, but a few visitors from the film industry stop in at the Whitney Store. Rich, famous, or not, everyone receives the same treatment—if a line has formed at the register, even celebrities must take their place at the end.

At the intersection of Movie Road and Whitney Portal Road,
a film crew sets up to shoot a commercial.

Two cooks in the kitchen: Doug Thompson, Jr. (left) and Eddie Salas. Eddie participated in the "Beyond Limits" program several years ago, and later became a Store employee.

"The cook in the hat is cute."
-8/21/99, Mammoth, CA

V. RECIPES FROM THE WHITNEY PORTAL KITCHEN

One day a gentleman came into the Store and asked a question. Doug, Jr. thought he said, "Where's the rest room?" so he gave the standard answer: across the pond. A few moments later, the man returned: "Not the rest room—the Restaurant!"

If you've eaten at the Whitney Store & Restaurant, you'll know that the Store IS the Restaurant. In fact, when

> *"Never had such a nice breakfast"*
> *-8/3/88, Holland*

Doug and Earlene bought the Store, they didn't realize how much food service was involved. When they discovered their new business included a busy restaurant, they adapted by learning and creating recipes that worked well.

Cooking for guests at 8,300'+ altitude has its challenges. Earlene laughs about it now, but she was near tears when one of the Store's first catastrophes happened. A customer ordered fried eggs for breakfast. Earlene heated up the griddle, and cracked open a fresh egg. The minute it hit the metal, the yolk broke. She tried

> *"Came all the way from 'Brooklyn New York' just to have a burger 'here' - took a lifetime"*
> *-7/25/00, San Diego, CA*

again, with the same outcome. After going through about 15 eggs, she was desperate. The customer was wondering why his eggs were taking so long to cook. Doug gave it a try, with the same explosive result. Finally, they explained the problem to the customer. Shrugging, he said he'd just take them scrambled.

> *"Great Cheesburgers"*
> *-7/8/88, Honolulu, HI*

After puzzling over the phenomenon, it was discovered that subjecting an egg to the temperature change (from very cold to very hot) at the high altitude was simply more stress than the yolk's membrane could bear. This explains why eggs "sunny side up" are not part of the breakfast fare.

For a time the restaurant's clientele came chiefly from the local towns, but the Thompsons eventually changed the menu to appeal more to campers and hikers. This also simplified their challenges of keeping adequate supplies on hand. The kitchen is open seven days a week during the season.

Most visitors eat at the outdoor tables, since indoor space is limited. The atmosphere and scenery outside outdoes any restaurant you've ever visited before, unless the weather is bad. The menu is small, but the food is unbeatably tasty, and portions are large

> *"The pancake was breathtaking (and the mountain wasn't bad either!)"*
> *-10/9/00, Laguna Niguel, CA*

enough to satisfy any hungry mountaineer. We've included a few favorites by popular demand. Try them in your own kitchen for a delicious reminder of your meals on the mountain.

For these recipes, you won't need your measuring spoons or cups. All you need is a sense of adventure—have fun!!

Doug Jr.'s Pancakes:

Approx. 4 cups
Krusteaz Pancake
mix
Add Warm water to
consistency of
muffin mix (very
thick). Do not
overmix; should be
lumpy
Pour in vanilla until
consistency is a bit
thinner, but still
thicker than cake
batter
Pour in cinnamon
We make these
BIG (average is
12-17 inches
across). Cook
on greased grill
or skillet at about
350 degrees.
One per person is usually plenty—they are very thick and
filling.

Ron Blanchette tackles a legend-
ary Whitney Store Pancake
(photo by Russell Simon)

The store
will let you have
them for free if
you can eat a
whole one. The
record is three pancakes at one sitting.

"I couldn't stop my husband from
eating your famous pancake!!!"
-9/25/00, San Diego, CA

We started a tradition with our pancakes to help out young families who couldn't afford an expensive meal. We would challenge them to eat a whole pancake, and if they could finish it we wouldn't charge them. We then tailored the size of the pancake to the size of the family--trying to make it big enough to fill them up but not too big that they couldn't finish it. We even had a T-shirt for awhile that said, "I ate the cake," for anyone who could eat the whole thing.

A Little Bit Different French Toast:

8 slices of bread—sourdough or wheat is best for this recipe.
4 eggs, whipped
A splash of orange juice
Cinnamon
Nutmeg
Vanilla

Cook on oiled grill or skillet until brown. This makes four servings.

Earlene's Chicken Breast Marinade:

Open your spice cupboard wide for this one!
2 cups orange juice
1/4 cup honey
1/2 cup barbecue sauce
1 onion cut into large pieces
3 large cloves
Crushed garlic
Fresh fruit pieces: orange, lemon, pineapple
Pour in herbs and spices—use your imagination and your nose! If you need some suggestions, try oregano, sage, Worcestershire sauce, and tarragon. Start out lightly—you can always add more.

Lightly puncture chicken breasts, marinate in mixture. We use frozen, skinless chicken and this recipe will marinate a lot. You may want to divide large portions of chicken into Ziploc bags, add a cup of marinade, and keep it in your freezer.

"Lovely place, great food"
-6/29/88, Kent, WA

Defrost **in the fridge** before grilling, sautéing, or baking (may also be broiled). Always cook chicken until meat is white at the thickest part and the juices are clear. Place some of the fruit pieces on chicken while it is cooking for a real treat. Cook as fast as possible so it doesn't dry up, but be sure it's done all the way through.

Doug Sr.'s Special Mountain Corn:

These ingredients sound odd together, but give it a try—
you'll be surprised!
1 large can of corn with liquid
1/4 cup honey
1/2 teaspoon cinnamon
2 tablespoons margarine or butter
Dash salt and pepper
Cook slowly until the water evaporates. Serve as a side
dish.

Prime Rib:

Garlic
Salt
Pepper
Lemon Pepper
Worcestershire sauce
Pesti's Italian Spaghetti Seasoning
Turn meat skin side up. Poke several holes and put 1/4
clove garlic into each one. Pat on salt, pepper, and other
spices. Best cooked in a kettle barbecue approx. 3 hours
for a whole Prime, but use a meat thermometer to be sure.
Oven method: roast approx. 3 hours at 325 degrees, or
until meat thermometer indicates 155 degrees in center of
largest area for about an hour. Ends should be well done
and center cuts will be medium to medium rare.

Barbecued Turkey:

Salt
Pepper
Sage
Onion
2 cups Orange Juice
Worcestershire sauce
Butter or Margarine
Lemon Pepper
Pesti's Italian Spaghetti Seasoning

Wash turkey inside and out with cold water. Empty
cavity, remove neck and giblets; save for soup (see next
page). Salt and pepper inside cavity, sprinkle with
sage, and place a whole, peeled onion inside. Splash
Worcestershire. Butter outside of bird and sprinkle
with salt, pepper, lemon pepper, and spaghetti seasoning. Cook in a kettle barbecue: 2-1/2 hours for a 12-
pound turkey. We always use a meat thermometer to
be safe: 170 degrees (internal).

*"This food passes my inspection!
-6/11/90, Independence, CA*

"Don't Throw That Carcass" Soup:

If parts of carcass are burned, break off and discard.

Salt
Pepper
Turkey Carcass, Neck and Giblets you saved
1 large Onion
4-5 Celery Stalks (with leaves)
4-5 Carrots
1 can Corn
2-3 large Potatoes
1/2 cup Tones brand chicken or turkey gravy mix
Celery salt
1/4 lb. pasta

In a large pot, cover carcass 2/3 with water. Add salt, pepper, neck and giblets. Bring to boil, simmer partially covered about one hour. In the meantime, chop onion, celery, and carrots into bite-size pieces and keep in cold water until broth is done. Chop unpeeled potatoes, parboil in salted water, and set aside. When broth is done, take out all meat and bone. Carefully remove meat from bones. We prefer to discard neck and giblets (and our dog prefers that too!). Add vegetables and meat to broth. Mix small amount of cold water into gravy mix and add to soup to thicken. Season soup with celery salt, pepper, or anything you like. Break pasta into 2-inch pieces, add to soup. Simmer about an hour. Add more Tones if it needs more flavor. Enjoy!

BIBLIOGRAPHY

Abbot, C. G., "A Shelter for Observers on Mount Whitney," *Smithsonian Miscellaneous Collections (Quarterly Issue)*, Vol. 52, Part 4, No. 1886. Washington, DC: Smithsonian Institution, January 12, 1910.

Bard, Allan, "Mt. Whitney: 14,495 Ft., East Buttress III, 5.7," *Shooting Star Guides*, Bishop, CA (undated).

Chapman, Robert D. and Brandt, John C., *The Comet Book: A Guide for the Return of Halley's Comet*, Boston: Jones and Bartlett Publishers, Inc., 1984.

Englander, William R., "Conquering the mountain in a day," *The San Diego Union-Tribune*, May 20, 1993.

Farquhar, Francis P., *History of the Sierra Nevada.* Los Angeles: University of California Press, 1965.

French, Harold, "The Highest House in America: How the New Observatory on Mt. Whitney Was Constructed," *San Francisco Chronicle*, November 7, 1909.

Graham, Tom, "The Drama of Mt. Whitney," *San Francisco Chronicle,* August 10, 1992.

Hellweg, Paul and McDonald, Scott, *Mount Whitney Guide for Hikers and Climbers.* Canoga Park, CA: Canyon Publishing Company, 1994.

Hopkins, Sarah Winnemucca. *Life Among the Piutes: Their Wrongs and Claims*, ed. by Mrs. Horace Mann. Las Vegas, NV: University of Nevada Press, 1994.

King, Clarence, *Mountaineering in the Sierra Nevada.* Lincoln, NE: University of Nebraska Press, 1970.

Langley, S. P. "Researches on Solar Heat and Its Absorption by the Earth's Atmosphere," U.S. War Department, Washington, DC: Government Printing Office, 1884.

Lone Pine Chamber of Commerce, "Lone Pine: Home of Mt. Whitney & Lone Pine Film Festival," January 1996.

Marsh, George F., "Gustave F. Marsh & Mount Whitney." Laguna Woods, CA: Personal research compiled and revised 22 December 2000.

Marsh, Gustave F., Letter to W. W. Campbell dated 5 June 1910. Archives of the Lick Observatory.

Mt. Whitney Store Guest Book, 1989-2001.

National Park Service, Division of Publications, *Sequoia and Kings Canyon: A Guide to Sequoia and Kings Canyon National Parks California.* Washington, DC: U.S. Department of the Interior, 1992.

Perez, Mary Anne, "Trouble Teen-Agers Weather Inhospitable Climbs," *Los Angeles Times*, August 14, 1991.

Putman, Jeff and Smith, Genny, ed., *Deepest Valley: A guide to Owens Valley, its roadsides and mountain trails.* Mammoth Lakes, CA: Genny Smith Books, 1995.

Putnam, George Palmer, *Up In Our Country.* New York: Duell, Sloan and Pearce, 1950.

Rowell, Galen, "The John Muir Trail: Along the High, Wild Sierra," *National Geographic*, Vol. 175, No. 4, April 1989, pp. 466-493.

Steward, Julian H., "Myths of the Owens Valley Paiute," *University of California Publications in American Archaeology and Ethnology*, Vol. 34, No. 5, pp. 355-440. Berkeley, CA: University of California Press, 1936.

Stone, Irving, "Desert Padre," *The Saturday Evening Post,* May 20, 1944.

Taliaferro, Charles R., *Mount Whitney Hiking Guide.* Independence, CA: High Sierra Adventures Trailhead Shuttle Service, 1986.

Wheelock, Walt and Condon, Tom, *Climbing Mount Whitney,* Fifth Edition. Glendale, CA: La Siesta Press, 1989.

Wood, Crispin Melton, "A History of Mount Whitney," Unpublished Thesis, College of the Pacific, 1955.

> *"It was worthwhile; the walk, the weight of our full packs, the beauty, the snow, the cold, the super Fantastic experience, etc."*
> *-10/15/00, Indonesia*

APPENDICES

APPENDIX A:
"This Year or Never," by Thomas A. LaRocca, August, 1979

APPENDIX B:
"The Highest House in America," by Harold French, November 7, 1909

APPENDIX C:
Letter to W. W. Campbell describing observations of Halley's Comet from the summit of Mount Whitney, by Gustave F. Marsh, June 5, 1910

APPENDIX D:
Lists of Flowers and Birds seen from Whitney Portal to Tulainyo Lake Overlook, by Marcyn Del Clements, March, 2002

APPENDIX E:
U.S. Congressional Record: "Celebrating the Rich History of Mt. Whitney," by Hon. Jerry Lewis, October 12, 1998

APPENDIX F:
"Timeless Mountain," by Elisabeth Newbold and Doug Thompson, November 25, 1999

● ●

APPENDIX A

"THIS YEAR OR NEVER"
by Thomas A. LaRocca
August, 1979

Authors' Note:

The authors chose to publish this personal account by Tom LaRocca for several reasons. It portrays a typical Mount Whitney experience, in that it describes the mental and physical preparation Tom went through before attempting to climb; it includes good examples of the interactions between hikers that take place as they move along the trail; it gives a clear schedule of events, including the time of day things occurred; it mentions some experience with altitude sickness; and it expresses emotions that most climbers feel as they undertake, conquer, and descend the peak.

Tom and his wife, Wilma, are former cabin owners who still enjoy trips up to the Portal, and maintain many friendships with other cabin residents. Even though this climb took place over 20 years ago, the experience is timeless enough that it is still a "textbook" example.

We express our gratitude to Tom and Wilma for their generosity in allowing us to share this writeup with you.

Tom signs the summit register while partner Will looks on (photo courtesy of Tom LaRocca)

"THIS YEAR OR NEVER"

This is my sixth year at our Whitney Portal cabin. I cannot count the number of times I have focused my sights and attention on the majestic and breathtaking peak that is Mt. Whitney. And each time I would ask myself the questions: Will I, and can I, climb to the top of Mt. Whitney?

I had heard many stories throughout the years of rescues made by helicopters and rescue teams, not only during the cold months, but also during the warm season. I had seen and talked with many hikers who had just finished their long trek. Mostly they had looked tired and had little to say. Some just couldn't wait to have a hamburger or an ice cream cone. And of course, I had heard the stories of many successful hikers.

Will I, and can I, climb to the top of Mt. Whitney, the highest peak in the continental United States, 14,495 feet? I had to find out. I made my big decision. This was the year, 1979, that I would attempt to do it. Now that my decision was made, there were more questions: What would be my strategy? How would I prepare myself? Knowing that I had to condition myself both physically and mentally, I set out to do this. And I worked hard at it. It is important to mention at this point that I wanted to make the climb and the descent in one day—a real challenge. Could I do it? I didn't know, but I had to find out.

Early in the season I hiked up the Meysan Trail alone— once in May and again in June. I didn't go very far—only to the first big waterfall (about two miles) and back. This was a good start in my conditioning process.

I don't like to hike alone, so I was fortunate in finding good hiking companions, new owners of a neighboring cabin, to accompany me on practice hikes. On Saturday, July 7, we started out to explore the Whitney Trail. Although we did not set out with any destination point in mind, we did rather well.

We went as far as the five-mile marker—Consultation Lake—returning home after seven hours. It was a good exercise in preparation, and we felt none the worse for it. I slept well that night and had no aches and pains the next morning. I hiked that day in Hush Puppy ankle boots, which I found to be light and supportive. They worked well for me.

Two weeks later, July 21, the three of us made our second climb up the Whitney Trail. This time I wore jogging shoes, which didn't work too well. I slipped while crossing a log. Luckily my foot was not injured—just very wet. This was hardly a deterrent, so we continued until we reached the six-mile marker at Trail Camp. We had gone one mile farther than our last hike, and we all felt strong. We knew that we had the stamina to continue on, but turned back downhill to attend a dinner we had been invited to that evening at another cabin. I was a bit tired, but slept well and felt fine the next morning.

I was fortified with the thought that if I was able to hike six miles up the Whitney Trail, why not eight miles, or even farther? I had high aspirations. After a trip back home to Alhambra Hills, I received a call from another friend and fellow cabin resident who had heard of my goal to climb Mt. Whitney. He had been jogging ten miles every night for a month to get into shape, and suggested a plan to do the big climb on Thursday, August 3. My practice hiking partners were not available on this date, so the two of us made arrangements to take a short hike on Tuesday, relax on Wednesday, and go the full distance on Thursday.

On Thursday, July 26, the day after my 58th birthday, my wife and I headed for the High Sierras once again. My friend arrived at the Portal Monday evening, July 30. Our practice hike on Tuesday was a steep scramble up the slope behind the cabins, where we reached one of the lower ridges after two and a half hours of fighting loose gravel. This was a great workout for our leg muscles. While we had planned to relax on Wednesday, we ended up helping haul a load of fir bark, pushing a wheelbarrow back and forth for part of the day. Again, this strengthened the muscles we would use the next day.

After a good dinner that evening, we planned what to wear the next day: long trousers, long-sleeved shirts, wide brimmed hats, and sun glasses. My friend decided to wear his hiking boots, and I went with my personal favorites, my Hush Puppy ankle boots. I went to bed early that night, full of anxieties and with that ever-present question: could I reach the summit of Mt. Whitney? I did not sleep well, suffering from stomach cramps. I had mixed feelings about this, but in the end I convinced myself that this distress was all for the better, since I would not have the cramps in the morning.

When the alarm rang the next morning at 3:45, I got quickly out of bed, feeling alert, happy and anxious. My stomach was fine. I ate a light breakfast of orange juice, puffed wheat, coffee, toast, and jam. I quickly packed my lunch: a sandwich, fruit, nuts, and candy. I walked down the hill to my friend's cabin, arriving at 4:45. He was ready, frisky and in good spirits. His Father drove us up to the foot of the trail, where we set out at 5:05 a.m. At long last we were on our way—and none too soon.

We were forced to use our flashlights the first ten minutes on the trail, but that was hardly an inconvenience. We found, to our surprise, that we were not the only ones on the trail at that hour, for we saw two young damsels several yards behind us. Were they in distress? By no means—they looked and acted as if they knew where they were coming from and where they were going. They were moving fast and traveling light. Our acquaintance with these young ladies turned out to be a fortunate event, as will become evident as this story progresses.

At the beginning of our climb I found myself perspiring and

gasping for breath. This continued for about two hours. I began to be concerned and was forced into some unpleasant reasoning: if I'm off to such a bad start, what will be the outcome? Will I eventually have to turn back? It seemed best not to let such doubts bother me. I did not make my feelings known to my companion. He could have moved at a much faster pace, I am sure, for he is taller, long-legged, and strong. He was sympathetic and kept up a pace which I could follow as he humored me along.

We encountered overnight campers at Lone Pine Lake, the first of the lakes along the Trail, about two and a half miles from Whitney Portal. They had just awakened and were moving about. We stopped to chat, and then moved on. At this point, I got my "second wind" and felt revitalized. The air was crisper and cooler. Feeling more comfortable and in a good state of mind, I took the lead position. We exchanged the lead position at will throughout the entire hike.

We arrived at Mirror Lake—10,000 feet altitude—at 7:30. We had completed the first four miles, and I would venture to say that they are the easiest for two reasons: first, it's a dirt trail up to this point; secondly, the grade isn't quite as steep. From Mirror Lake on it's granite rock all the way to the summit and the climb becomes steeper and more difficult. In spite of these hazards we did not slow down or stop for breath. Our young lady friends passed us along the way—I don't remember exactly at what point—but I would guess it was somewhere after Mirror Lake. Before they passed, we conversed with them and learned they were from Illinois and were presently students at USC. My friend borrowed their suntan lotion, after which they proceeded on their way.

We arrived at Trailside Meadow at 8:15. This is the five-mile mark. It's quite pretty, with little purple flowers scattered along the streams and small birds begging for crumbs. We rested here for a few minutes and drank several cupfuls of ice cold running water. How refreshing it was!

We continued our steep climb and arrived at Trail Camp, 12,000 feet altitude, at 9:15. From here we could look down into Consultation Lake, the biggest of all the lakes on the Whitney Trail. From this viewpoint it looked cold and uninviting. There was no ice or snow around it, however. We saw campsites, colorful tents, and hikers milling about—a very impressive sight indeed!

After leaving Trail Camp came the true test. I had hiked to this point once before with my friends—all well and good. Could I surpass my previous mark? I was certain that I could. I felt strong and sure-footed. The next two miles were the well-known—perhaps more accurately termed infamous—one hundred switchbacks. Are there really a hundred of them? I don't know, but someone must have counted them. We were well above timberline now, and all we could see around us was granite rock and big patches of snow alongside the switchbacks. I had no problem climbing these; neither did my friend. Water was plentiful in this area, with streams passing over and under the Trail.

Before long we could see the top of the ridge, but we were still a long way off. I was becoming very anxious. My friend kept my spirits up by telling me that it was just a matter of minutes. We then met a very weary hiker, which gave us an excuse to stop, rest, and chat. We learned that he was just starting his three-week trek. On his back was a sixty-five-pound pack! He took out a cigarette, lit it, and then breathed a sigh of relief. He remarked that he would not smoke while hiking. This young man has passed through my thoughts many times since, and I have wondered if his three-week trip was a success. He seemed unprepared mentally and physically for such a long journey. We wished him God-speed and left.

At approximately 11:00 a.m. we arrived at Trail Crest Pass, 13,777 feet altitude. The view now was breathtaking, beyond description. For the first time we could see the other side—the western slope—Sequoia National Forest. We decided that this was the place to have lunch, since there was plenty of atmosphere and scenic beauty. The winds were a bit strong and gusty, but it didn't matter. I made a feeble attempt at eating. I really wasn't hungry, but managed to eat half a sandwich, a tomato, and a small bunch of grapes. This satisfied me. My friend, on the other hand, was famished and ate two sandwiches. We rested awhile, and soon realized that an hour had passed. It was noon and we still had two and a half miles to go.

The next half-mile was easy, for it was all downhill—a kind of misleading introduction to what was to come. In about fifteen minutes we reached the John Muir Trail Junction. Here we ran into (not to be taken literally) about six hikers coming up from Sequoia, from whom we learned that another hiker from Sequoia was in trouble on the trail below. The best we could gather was that he needed assistance and that a friend was helping him carry his pack. We could see them coming up the trail ever so slowly. In the meantime a hiker—and a good samaritan indeed—was heading down the trail. He was trying to get word through that someone was in trouble. Not until later was this episode resolved for us.

At the Junction I started out before my partner. This was a mistake, for I took the wrong trail. It would have taken me into Sequoia National Forest. Then came my friend's loud question: "Where do you think you're going?" I turned around and followed him, as he chided me a bit. We had now covered 8.7 miles—just another two miles to go. Could I do it? I knew I could. I felt good and strong. According to my hiking companion, this was the part of the journey where you walk fifty yards and stop to catch your breath. He wasn't far from wrong, even though he had exaggerated somewhat. When he got too far ahead of me, I would shout out to him, "Remember your words—every fifty yards we stop—right?" And we would both chuckle as he good-naturedly waited for me.

About a mile before the summit we began to pass hikers who had reached it and were making their descent. We came across a troop of boy scouts—some looked no older than nine or ten—and some looked ill. The altitude had taken its toll. As we moved closer still, we could see the two pinnacles beside Mt. Whitney. As we passed on the trail between them, I had all I could do with keeping both feet on the trail and keeping myself balanced. It was a sheer drop on both sides of the trail. I found this portion of the trail to be dangerous and treacherous, and we were crossing it in the most ideal of conditions.

The back side of Mt. Whitney has an entirely different appearance than the front. It is well-rounded, whereas the front side is pointed and jagged. My friend kept up his words of encouragement to me, and tried to point out the stone house at the summit, but I could not see it. A pair of hikers who passed at this point must have seen the weary and forlorn look in my eyes. They encouraged me with their smiles and their comment, "You're there now!" These words gave me new vigor. We pushed on and finally arrived at the stone house at 1:40 p.m.

Yes, the hour of glory and fulfillment had come. I felt like singing out a thousand 'alleluias. What a tremendous and overpowering feeling it was to know that I was on top of the world, at least here in the continental United States.

It is customary that one sign the register outside the stone hut. This I was very happy to do. I asked my friend to take a photo of me standing by the register. Another climber nearby overheard this request and offered to take a picture of both of us by the register. I hoped that this shot especially would come out.

After the signing in we advanced straight ahead, toward the side facing Whitney Portal and the Owens Valley. Soon we realized that our young lady friends had made it up before us. As we sat and chatted, they mentioned that one of them had been ill on the way up and was still feeling queasy. They left the summit to make their descent at 2:15. We were destined to meet these girls one more time later on.

We planned to spend an hour or more on the summit, leaving at 3:00 p.m. This would give us ample time to absorb the majestic beauty of Mt. Whitney's peak. As we sat facing the Owens Valley, munching grapes, tiny birds flitted about after the seeds. I was surprised to see these little beggars at this altitude.

After awhile, my partner stretched out under a long rock to avoid the sun and took a nap. I, on the other hand, started a conversation with the same gentleman who had snapped our picture by the register. He was very informative, and happy to explain what we saw before us—peaks, passes, lakes, and forests. He knew the country well. This is easy to understand, for besides being an experienced teacher, he was also a scouting coordinator who had hiked the High Sierras for a good many years.

Time was moving along; already it was 3:15. It was time to make our descent, but my friend was nowhere in sight. I searched for fifteen minutes, calling out his name. Naturally I began to wonder about his disappearance. Horrible thoughts passed through my mind—had he fallen off a ledge? I saw a stone enclosure in the distance which aroused my curiosity, so I walked over in its direction. It had no roof. As I approached, I could see an opening. With a sigh of relief, I found him inside.

Needless to say, he had fallen victim to the altitude. I sympathized with him. He took two aspirin and then courageously expressed a wish to move on. We were somewhat behind schedule, but we knew we could make up the time on our descent.

After two hours my companion was feeling better. His fast pace told me as much. After a mile or so down the trail we saw a rescue helicopter overhead. We knew that it was not just passing by, that it was definitely searching for someone in distress. Immediately we concluded that it had to be the person needing assistance back at the Junction. About three hours had passed, and we were now heading down the switchbacks. The helicopter continued to weave in and out of our mountain range. It was very interesting to watch the pattern of its flight. We had to wonder if at any point it would land, and finally it did. We were about three quarters of the way down the switchbacks when we saw the helicopter on the ground at Trail Camp with several people alongside it.

We arrived at Trail Camp about 5:30. By that time the helicopter had already taken off and returned to its base. The best information we could gather was that the person supposedly in distress had not wanted to be flown in for medical aid. He claimed he could make it on his own. We discussed the high costs of flying in a chopper these days, and who would be obligated to pay for this service.

As we made our way through Trail Camp, we observed lots of activity. Here was a small community—about thirty or forty hikers—young and old, busily moving about. Tents had already been pitched, stoves were burning, and some hungry campers were already eating their evening meal. Everyone was high-spirited and, I'm sure, anxious for what was to come the following day. We were greeted with big smiles as we passed through, and found it easy to chat with some of these campers.

We still had six more miles ahead of us, but fortunately it was all downhill. This was very consoling. We quickened our pace and at times went into a running walk. We kept this up till we reached the end of the trail at Whitney Portal. It was now 8:20, and somewhat dark. For me, thirst was more of a factor than anything else. The first thing I wanted was a cold soda pop, so we stopped at the Portal Store.

Continuing on, we soon heard welcome voices from the parking lot. Once again it happened that two gentlemen met the two damsels—who were not in distress. This was providential. The girls remarked that they had come off the trail only five minutes before us, and that they were about to look for a campsite for the night. When I mentioned that we still had another mile to walk to our cabins, I definitely had an ulterior motive. The girls offered to drop us off at our cabins, for which we were grateful.

Several weeks have passed since I conquered the summit of Mt. Whitney in one day. I have had time to reflect on the wonderful vistas and to evaluate this whole deep and satisfying experience. I have often been asked the question: would you do it again? My answer is definitely in the affirmative, for I know now that each time I climb the highest peak in the "lower 48" it will be a thrilling and spiritually rewarding journey. I began with the thought of doing it once in my lifetime—of achieving it being a this-year-or-never-proposition. I know now that climbing Mt. Whitney is too wonderful to remain just a one-time event in my memory. I want to do it again, because I know that each trip will offer different sights, new experiences, and a chance for me to feel once again the awesome power that comes with being on top of the world.

Summit shelter 1911 - Campbell's horizontal telescope in foreground (photo courtesy of George Marsh)

APPENDIX B

THE HIGHEST HOUSE IN AMERICA: HOW THE NEW OBSERVATORY ON MT. WHITNEY WAS CONSTRUCTED
San Francisco Chronicle, Sunday, November 7, 1909
by
Harold French
(printed verbatim, with original spelling)

Cemented to a granite foundation, 14,501 feet above sea level, a class A, fire and earthquake proof structure of stone and steel now crowns the crest of Mount Whitney, the highest point in the United States. The observatory was constructed late last August by the Smithsonian Institution, represented by Dr. Abbot, director of the Mount Wilson observatory, with the co-operation of Professor Alexander G. MacAdie of the United States Weather Bureau and Dr. Campbell, director of Lick Observatory. Concerning it, the latter of these noted men of science says: It is a great credit to the Smithsonian Institution and to the superintendent of the construction, G. F. Marsh, a public-spirited citizen of Lone Pine, who struggled, valiantly and successfully against the difficulties of transporting cement and steel to the summit, as well as difficulties of less open character. Marsh's connection with the project is one in which he is entitled to feel the utmost pride, and I trust that his fellow citizens of Lone Pine and Inyo County will appreciate his services in this connection.

Important as is the scientific value of this unique observatory, its deeper human interest lies in the heroic efforts of the men who blazed the trail. Indeed, the building of this citadel of science might have been indefinitely deferred were it not for the perseverance of a man with a high ideal. For eight long, discouraging years his fixed purpose of life was to accomplish the erection of an observatory on the summit of Mount Whitney, having the faith and foresight to realize what a great advantage such an attraction would be to his community, for whose betterment he labored. With a few resolute companions, he struggled with the elements far up that savage Sierran scarp, and by his force of character overcame the more insidious obstacles of jealousy and doubt which beset his path below. How these men of tried steel hewed their way through barriers of granite and ice, is a story for the pen of a Kipling to relate. Readers of realistic fiction who have reveled in The Bridge Builders or Caleb West, Master Diver, would find the facts regarding the building of the Lone Pine trail and the dream of the observatory fulfilled a volume of even more tensely thrilling interest.

PEOPLE OF LONE PINE PAVE WAY.

An eagle soaring from the summit of Mount Whitney toward the sunrise fourteen miles in an air line would glance nearly eleven thousand feet directly down upon the little town of Lone Pine. For more than a third of a century it has slumbered peacefully in the secluded valley of the Owens River, which skirts the eastern foothills of the Sierra for 100 miles down to the dead sea of California, Owens Lake. Then new blood revived these isolated towns of Inyo, and, following certain enterprising newcomers, came a railroad which will soon carry out the produce of Owens Valley. Twenty streams pouring forth from the Sierran snowfields are now being harnessed for the generation of more than 100,000 horse-power, while the water is being diverted to the rich valley soil with a degree of success that is repeating the history of irrigation in Southern California. Among these desirable citizens came an Englishman, Gustave F.

Marsh, who, after investigating the opportunities of other districts of the awakening West, decided to share in the development of Inyo County.

He located in Lone Pine, and eight years ago joined with other progressive residents of Inyo County in agitating a popular sentiment in favor of building a pack trail to the summit of the mountain. With few exceptions the people of Lone Pine perceived that the construction of a safe trail up Mount Whitney would attract scientists to the summit, and that their influence might induce the Government to establish an observatory there, which would naturally bring their town into prominence. In August, 1903, Messrs. Spears, Cross and Spears, together with the photographer, Harvey, returned from a reconnoitering trip over the proposed route. Their reports were so favorable that the sum of $700 was promptly subscribed for the purpose of outfitting a party of fourteen, who, under the direction of Mr. Spears, constructed the trail up through the foaming canyon of Lone Pine creek, past the picturesque Lake of the Lonesome Pine to the pass of the same romantic name at an elevation of 13,000 feet. Although within three and one-half miles of the summit, the pioneer party was compelled to abandon the work because the funds had become exhausted.

The heroic and herculean task of carving a course, through granite ice and avalanche-accumulating slide rock was far more difficult and expensive than bargained for, and all who have struggled with the overwhelming forces of nature under similar circumstances will appreciate the disappointment of these men, who returned only when their supplies gave out.

It was at this juncture that the people of Inyo County rallied to the support of the project, and the Supervisors appropriated the sum of $200 to enable the trail builders to complete their work. Marsh was chosen to lead the second party, and although late in the season he started up with fifteen men, of whom seven deserted during the first few days. It was late in October, and at an elevation of two miles and a half the wind was bitterly cold, as it surged savagely around the dizzy cliffs. Sleet and icy rain beat down upon them, while avalanches would repeatedly obliterate their new-made trail. The sliding talus was treacherous, and when the men would blast a bowlder out of their path they would see, to their dismay, tons of rough angular rocks roll down into their path. It was heartbreaking work lifting these heavy masses, thousands and thousands of them, when the rarefied air of this high altitude made physical effort most fatiguing.

Although the thin atmosphere produced violent headaches and afflicted them with nausea, they nevertheless toiled on and upward. A huge barrier of ice and snow they bridged by throwing dirt and gravel upon its surface and packing it down until animals could pass over it in safety. In places it was necessary to blast through jutting ledges and the overhanging ramparts rang with the roar of the detonating dynamite. They buttressed the downward side of the trail with dovetailing bowlders of granite and lava and crammed the crevices with fragments of rubble until the footing was secure for the pack-laden horses and mules. Finally, on October 30th a blinding snowstorm proved the last straw. All day long they toiled with dogged desperation, despite the fact that they could barely distinguish one another, so thick and fast fell the flakes. After a long and bitter night, exposed to the fury of the storm, without a tent for shelter, they realized that they would be snowed in hopelessly if they lingered, and with the dawn they cached their tools and returned to Lone Pine, bitterly disappointed, but not discouraged.

"ONCE MORE UNTO THE BREACH."
Winter descended with all its rigors upon Mount Whitney,

220

but the builders of the trail were far from hibernating down in the pleasant valley of the Owens. Three hundred dollars were required to complete the trail and the ladies of Lone Pine came to the front with the tidy sum of $69 netted from a basket social and dance, while the neighboring towns of Independence and Keeler contributed the generous sums of $85 and $67 respectively. Other residents of Inyo swelled the fund with hard-earned coin at considerable personal sacrifice in some cases, while many proffered their labor for a number of days for the common good of their county.

On July 8, 1904, the third expedition went to the front in the best of spirits and with the determination to win. Its members found the trail in excellent condition until they reached Mexican Camp, their base of supplies, 12,000 feet above the sea. Here their troubles began, and their animals broke through the snow. It became necessary to shovel a trench for 300 yards through the deep drift until they could lead the animals up to Lone Pine pass. In many places they were obliged to carry the packs on their own backs in order to encourage the skeptical and pessimistic mules. Firewood was carried up to a new camp at the elevation of 13,552 feet. From this point upward for the remaining thousand feet the men vied with one another to complete their allotted strips first. In the van proceeded the drillers, who blasted their way round hitherto impassable cliffs. When within but a few hundred yards of the summit they came upon a chasm which it seemed no human foot could cross. "We're done beat now for sure," the men groaned when they beheld the precipitous cliff, but Marsh only smiled and set the dynamite to work reducing the angle of the cliff until the gap was bridged with debris. At last, on the 17th of July, the builders of the trail had finished their work, and with a cheer the first pack train trampled the flat roof of Whitney. The packs consisted of pitch pine, rockets, and dynamite, and that night the watchers down in Lone Pine saw their beloved mountain transformed into a volcano, as the signal fire flamed from its crest and the salvos of dynamite rumbled down the gorges.

THEN THE OBSERVATORY.

For four years the trail served the worthy purpose of attracting increasing numbers of mountain lovers to Lone Pine. They ascended its scenic and sinuous curves past roaring cataracts to the placid Lone Pine and Mirror lakes, where gamy trout abide and abound. Government scientists scaled the summit from its now most accessible side, and determined its exact elevation to be 14,501 feet. In the summer of 1908 Mr. Marsh took Professors Abbot and Campbell, directors of the Mount Wilson and Lick observatories respectively, up to the summit of Mount Whitney on a tour of investigation. They were strongly impressed with the flat roof of the mountain as a splendid site for an observatory, and found the conditions of dry and clear atmosphere most favorable to important research work. In 1881 Professor Langley, the father of the aeroplane, camped for a number of weeks 3000 feet below the summit, conducting a series of experiments which enabled him to calculate the solar constant, or the total amount of heat the earth would receive from the sun if the atmosphere did not absorb a large percentage of its radiant energy.

Fifteen years ago Dr. Campbell had visited Mount Whitney and, realizing that its crest was above four-fifths of the moisture in the earth's atmosphere, he foresaw the value to science of a series of spectrographic photographs, which would determine the amount of water vapor in the atmosphere of our neighbor planets, particularly Mars. During all these years he warmly indorsed the project of establishing a shelter on this mountain top, where scientists may place their delicate apparatus and study the unsolved problems of astronomy, astro-physics, meteorology, biology and other kindred subjects. Now that the public-spirited people of Lone Pine had demonstrated the practicability of transporting building materials, supplies of all kinds and even the most delicate instruments with comparative safety to this lofty look-out ledge, the way was paved for the planning of the observatory that would crown their efforts with success. Dr. Abbot, representing the Smithsonian Institution, informed Mr. Marsh that a fund would be appropriated for this purpose if he would assure the officials in Washington that the trail would be put in first-class condition. Mr. Marsh agreed to his part, and secured, as the lowest bidder, the contract for packing some fourteen tons of cement, sand, steel, glass and other supplies to the summit during the ensuing summer.

BUILDING THE OBSERVATORY.

Five winters had wrapped white blankets around the frost-sculptured form of Whitney. Avalanches and storms had played ninepins with the trail, and once more the call for contributions came to the good people of Lone Pine and its altruistic neighbors. Again the ladies of Lone Pine came to the front with their choicest cakes, pies and other toothsome temptations. They served a savory supper after a merry dance, a happy combination which proved the event of the season. The population of Lone Pine is but 350, yet they cleared $130 that evening by charging the moderate rate of $1.50 a couple. The lemonade stand proved a bonanza, for its clean-up was just $13.90, while Independence and Keeler once more added their quota.

On the 18th of last July Marsh attacked the snow drifts above the timber line with a force of men, who with axes and grubbing-hoes hewed a path for the pack train to follow. For two days following the party was crippled with snow blindness, the torture of which is most excruciating; yet with masks made from gunny saks the men still labored on until the arrival of colored glasses relieved their torment. At 13,550 feet they were obliged to build a quarter of a mile of new trail in order to wind around a field of soft snow, while the work of reconstructing the old way required the frequent use of dynamite. Blinding head-aches, extreme exhaustion resulting from hard manual labor in such rarefied air, all these were their daily portion. Once more the funds gave out and an increasing demand for labor down in the valley lured some of the men from the heights. A few, however, remained with Marsh to the last, when, on the 28th of July, the nimble-footed mules finally stood silhouetted against the indigo sky that hangs seemingly close to the summit.

As soon as the long-eared collaborators were relieved of their burdens, the foundation was commenced. A camp was established in a sheltered cranny where a supply of firewood accumulated. Snow was melted on pieces of sheetiron roofing and the water used to mix with cement. Walls of re-enforced concrete rose rapidly upward. Then came a terrifying thunderstorm, and Marsh was deserted by the last of his men. Alone on the summit he set his teeth and with unflinching grit decided to complete the observatory single handed, but after two days his helpers returned and finished their work. On the 29th of last August, this pioneer building was ready to serve its purpose as a shelter for scientific expeditions. It is thirty feet in length, twelve in width and ten in height, and is divided into three rooms, one of which will remain unlocked as "a shelter in the time of storm" for the accommodation of tourists. It is hoped that this favor will be appreciated by all who may seek refuge in this life-saving station on the peak, where decades ago John Muir danced all night to keep from freezing.

An expedition from Lick Observatory was financed last August by a Regent of the University of California, and Dr. W. W. Campbell was chosen to lead the party, which consisted of several from Mount Hamilton, Dr. Miller of San Jose and

Professor MacAdie of the Weather Bureau. The party left Lone Pine on August 28th, and after spending two days at Lone Pine lake in order to become acclimated to the altitude, they joined Dr. Abbot, the director of the Smithsonian Institution Observatory, whom they found engaged in a remarkably thorough study of the intensity of the solar radiation.

Dr. Campbell transported a sixteen-inch horizontal-reflecting telescope with spectroscopic attachments, with which he made certain discoveries of great astronomical importance. He demonstrated the absence of water vapor in appreciable quantities in the atmosphere of Mars by means of photographing its spectrum. Had water been present to the slightest extent, the solar rays passing through the atmosphere of Mars and being reflected to the earth would have shown a distant dark band on the photographic plate. Only the faintest vapor band was revealed by the spectroscope in the analysis of the light rays traversing the Martian atmosphere, and even this could be attributed to the small percentage of moisture in the atmosphere of our earth still suspended above the summit of Whitney. The result of this discovery would tend to refute the canal theory of Schiaparelli and those of the yellow journal scientific contributors, who still maintain that life, such as we know, exists in a waterless atmosphere.

FUTURE SCOPE OF OBSERVATORY.

Professor MacAdie, the meteorologist who accompanied the Campbell party, was one of the first and most ardent advocates of Mount Whitney as an observatory site, because of its accessibility, clear sky and its elevation above the water vapor of lower levels. On his recent visit he spent seven nights on the summit where he studied the phenomena of the upper air from a most favorable vantage point. As a meteorological station where the laws of storms may be studied and the changes of temperature and barometric pressure may be better understood. Mount Whitney will add greatly to the knowledge of a devoted corps of Government scientists who desire to apply the facts they will learn to the daily needs of the farmer folk down in the valleys below. The observatory will doubtless attract the more progressive men of science who will take advantage of its opportunities for research work along the lines of their respective specialties, and in the course of the next few years it will probably be enlarged to accommodate the pilgrims to this mountain-Mecca.

WHAT WHITNEY OVERLOOKS.

One can never imagine the majesty of this mountain until he sees with his own eyes the grandeur of the sunrise. Six thousand feet sheer, the titanic fault scarp falls away to the dun and drab foothills at its base. Grotesque pinnacles and the eerie and weirdly-carved crags burn red above the spotless whiteness of the snowfields. Below for a hundred miles the Owens' valley drains into its saline sea. Its floor, however, is a green oasis, where the magic touch of water is transforming 1000 square miles of grazing land into highly productive orchards and vineyards. The raisin grape is becoming a popular favorite among these ranchers of Inyo, whose dry climate guarantees the successful curing of the sugary crop. Half-way up the savage saw-toothed slopes the eagle soars over forests of fox-tail pine and shaggy tamaracks, and sees his image reflected in countless crystal lakes whose foaming outlets are ordained to turn the wheels of future industries.

Beyond the green gladness of the Owens vale, the mineralized Inyo mountains swell, and over them still the painted Panamints pierce the sky over toward the great mysterious desert, where stretch the sunken sandy wastes of Death Valley seventy fathoms below the level of Balboa's sea.

• •

APPENDIX C

LETTER TO W. W. CAMPBELL DESCRIBING OB-SERVATIONS OF HALLEY'S COMET FROM THE SUMMIT OF MOUNT WHITNEY
(edited version, with some original spelling & punctuation)
June 5, 1910
by
Gustave F. Marsh

Lone Pine, California   5 June 1910

Prof W. W. Campbell, Mt. Hamilton

Dear Sir,

Your kind letter to hand Friday night. . . . (answering your inquiry about my observations of Halley's Comet from the summit of Mt. Whitney last May.) I was very anxious to see the building & so many promised to go with me but they all fell down at the last minute. So I determined to go alone for J. E. Church kindly loaned me snowshoes. So I started Sunday morning 8:30 & figured to be on the top at 12 AM next day & see the Comet & Eclipse. I drove to the power plant & started to walk at 12 AM. I took 1 Blanket, 1 piece of Canvas, some tea & coffee, 1 can Baked bean, snow shoes & 1/2 pint whiskey. It made quite a load. I took my time & got to Lone Pine Lake 4:20 & Robinson's Camp at 5 PM. First snow at 10000 ft., trail all good so far with small patches of snow off and on to timber line.

I fixed my camp, built a big fire, gathered up all the old sacks I could find & old clothes & made me a pretty good bed with some boxes for a wind break. I passed the night very comfortable. I got up at 3 AM, ate my breakfast & started out just as it was light enough, about 4 AM. The Snow was just right for traveling. No frost at Robinson's Camp. I made good time to that first big snow bank. There the snow was so hard I could not get a footing. My snow shows would not hold so I took to the rocks & with my snow shoes & pack it was quite a task, but I did fine. It was good going till I got to about 12,500 about where the ice was last year. There I found the snow very hard and smooth, that was about 6 AM.

I could not use my snow shoes, so I used them to dig holes for my feet. I found that was very difficult, I needed an alpine stock then. I had to stamp my feet down till I got a footing & the higher I got the worse it got & I dare not turn round, so I made a bee line for the cliffs towards the east but oh my it was so slow. I had to make sure of every step, but I made it in safety. At Lone Pine side I never saw the snow so smooth & hard & it was easy going to Lake View Camp. From there, there was very little snow till I got to the big bank near Mt. Whitney, but it was easy going. I got to the top at 11:15 oh but I was tired.

I made a fire & started my can of beans for soup. Took out the mirror & at 12 noon I signaled to Lone Pine & got an answer in 3 minutes. I had promised my wife I would signal at 12. After I got an answer I felt pretty good. I ate my bean soup, sat out in the sun, looked around & saw a big fat ground Hog sitting by the monument. He did not seem a bit afraid, he came & packed off some old bread I had thrown out.

I found the building in good shape, only the door to the room for the tourist was down & the room was half full of snow & it's pretty sure someone did not fasten it very well or left it

228

open entirely. It can be put back in a few minutes with help. Quite a bit of snow had drifted in the other two rooms through the door ventilators & laps in the roof. I find it will be necessary to close up every crevice.

There was no snow on top of the mountain. It was a beautiful day & I got ready to see the comet, but at 5 PM it got cloudy, but the moon came up full speed alright & was clear as a bell, but towards night it clouded again & for the first quarter of the moon it was cloudy, but after that it was clear.

The comet was in plain view as soon as it was dark & just before the moon was covered the sky was perfectly clear except the fog bank very low down towards Visalia & the comet showed up grand & was in plane sight until the head of the comet got in the fog bank it seemed particularly bright at about 8:30 when the moon was almost covered the tail almost reached the moon, it swept almost across the sky.

I slept good. I had quite a headache at times. I made a signal fire at night & saw 5 fires in return. The minimum temperature was 23 degrees below zero & max 55 (as recorded by McAdie's thermometers left there last September). There was 10% frost the night of the 23rd. At 5 PM it was 36 & at 7 AM it was 22. I left the top at 7 AM & got home in town at 2:30. I found it more difficult coming down the snow on the Lone Pine side than it was going up, but I kept on the rocks all I could. I slipped once but did not slide very far.

I was very tired for days. Hoping to see you again soon. I shall be glad to introduce you to Maule Whitney Marsh born March 21st.
Best Love to all from us all
Yours Truly, G. F. Marsh

Alpine Gold (Hulsea algida)
(photo by Marcyn Del Clements)

● ●

APPENDIX D

LISTS OF FLOWERS AND BIRDS
SEEN FROM WHITNEY PORTAL
TO TULAINYO LAKE OVERLOOK
by Marcyn Del Clements
March, 2002

Introduction to Lists:

When Doug Thompson from the Portal Store led me up the Mountaineer's route in June 2000, into the Carillon mesas (called for the prominent peak to the west) and up to the over-look of Tulainyo Lake, I was exhausted but awestruck. Not only was this fishless lake starkly beautiful, at 12,802 feet a.s.l., but hardly anyone ever came here, especially not by the way we climbed, up through the mesas.

I was so enchanted by this place and the thought that Indians had been here and stayed, that I made a second pilgrimage all alone a month later.

Doug and I were interested in what was blooming. Being an amateur naturalist, I always want to name things and look things up. He encouraged me to make a list.

It was interesting to me that when we hiked up in June, it was full summer for the flowers, but when I climbed up barely over a month later, in August, it was already turning fall in the high country, with the Rabbitbrush blooming and many more flowers in the Sunflower Family.

I'd like to mention that this entire route is not for the faint of heart! But if you go there, following Doug's instructions, you too may feel the presence of ancient peoples before you; you too may feel the enchantment.

-Marcyn Del Clements, 1 March 2002

A LIST OF FLOWERS SEEN ON PORTAL TO TULAINYO LAKE OVERLOOK

as seen on June 27-28, 2000
(possible & probable)

Compiled by Marcyn Del Clements, with research assistance from my husband, Richard F. Clements.
Order based on the field guide: *Sierra Nevada Wildflowers* by Elizabeth L. Horn.

BUCKWHEAT FAMILY
Eriogonum species, poss. *nudum* (dry slopes)
Oxyria digyna, Mountain Sorrel (sheltering next to rocks)

BUTTERCUP FAMILY
Aquilegia formosa, Crimson Columbine (Flower Garden, named by Doug Thompson - a mesic area below the Carillon outfall)

CARROT FAMILY
Heracleum lanatum, Cow Parsnip (in Fern Wood, also called Cedar Grove, at very beginning above main Mt. Whitney trail)
Sphenosciadium capitellum, Ranger's Buttons (Flower Garden)

EVENING PRIMROSE FAMILY
Epilobium angustifolium, Fireweed (Flower Garden & elsewhere)
Castilleja species, poss. *miniata*, Indian Paintbrush (mesic areas)

FIGWORT FAMILY
Penstemon davidsonii, Davidson's Penstemon (dry slopes)
Penstemon rydbergii, Meadow Penstemon

GENTIAN FAMILY
Gentianopsis holopetala, Sierra Fringed Gentian (Flower Garden)

GOOSEBERRY FAMILY
Ribes species, both Currant and Gooseberry. (Gooseberries have spines, Currants do not.) (along the slopes)
HEATH FAMILY
Ledum glandulosum, Labrador Tea
Phyllodoce breweri, Red Heather (esp. in ravine near Indian Camp)
Sarcodes sanguinea, Snow Plant (very beginning, Fern Wood)
IRIS FAMILY
Sisyrinchium bellum, Blue-Eyed Grass
LEGUME FAMILY
Lupinus species, Lupine
OAK FAMILY
Chrysolepis sempervirens, Bush Chinquapin (ubiquitous)
PHLOX FAMILY
Ipomopsis aggregata, Scarlet Gilia
Polemonium eximium, Sky Pilot (only end of route, above mesas)
PRIMROSE FAMILY
Dodecatheon jeffreyi, Jeffrey Shooting Star
Primula suffrutescens, Sierra Primrose (up high, on way to overlook)
PURSLANE FAMILY
Calyptridium umbellatum, Pussypaws
Claytonia perfoliata, Miner's Lettuce (first stream crossing)
ROSE FAMILY
Cercocarpus ledifolius, Curl-Leaf Mountain Mahogany
Chamaebatia foliolosa, Mountain Misery
Rosa woodsii, Wood's Rose (Flower Garden)
STONECROP FAMILY
Sedum rosea, Western Roseroot, or Rosy Sedum (higher up, cliff-side)

SUNFLOWER FAMILY
Aster alpigenus, Alpine Aster
Erigeron species, prob. *pygmaeus*, Dwarf Daisy
Hulsea algida, Alpine Gold or Alpine Hulsea (at overlook to Tulainyo)
VIOLET FAMILY
Viola adunca, Western Long-spurred Violet

Added to list (or confirmed) from Solo trip on August 14-15, 2000 (From Portal to "Indian Encampment" only) Also reflects not only new insights, but changes in what is now blooming, over what was blooming a month ago. - MDC

BUCKWHEAT FAMILY
Eriogonum nudum, Nude Buckwheat (for sure, especially up on Carillon mesas in the dry slopes)
BUTTERCUP FAMILY
Actaea rubra, Baneberry (at first stream crossing & again in mesic area above Lower Boy Scout Lake)
EVENING PRIMROSE FAMILY
Epilobium canum, California Fuchsia (along dry slopes, especially on the overhanging seep north of Lower Boy Scout Lake)
Castilleja applegatei, Applegate Paintbrush (on dry slopes)
Castilleja miniata, Indian Paintbrush (in the meadows)
FIGWORT FAMILY
Mimulus guttatus, (Slimy-leaved) Monkeyflower (at overhang seep)
Penstemon rostriflorus, Bridge's Penstemon (Flower Garden)
LEGUME FAMILY
Lupinus latifolius, Broad-leaved Lupine (Flower Garden)

MINT FAMILY
Stachys albens, White Hedgenettle (Fern Woods a.k.a. Cedar Grove)
ROSE FAMILY
Ivesia santolinoides, Mousetails (all over Indian Camp area on mesas, a miniscule flower but with furry soft leaves)
SAXIFRAGE FAMILY
Heuchera rubescens, Alumroot (Carillon mesas, sheltered in rocks)
SUNFLOWER FAMILY
Achillea millefolium, Yarrow (dry slopes)
Chrysothamnus nauseosus, Rubber Rabbitbrush (late bloomer) [possibly Ericameria too, but I didn't distinguish them - that's the trouble with being an amateur]
Helenium bigelovii, Bigelow Sneezeweed (Flower Garden, and an interesting dwarf form at the streamside on the mesas. Are they the same?)
Senecio triangularis, Arrowleaf Butterweed (Indian Camp, streamside)
Solidago multiradiata, Alpine Goldenrod (same place, growing along stream in that meadow on the Carillon Mesa)

Note on trees: both Whitebark Pine (*Pinus albicaulis*) and Foxtail Pine (*Pinus balfouriana*) were present at my Indian Camp on the Carillon Mesa. I found the small cones with incurved prickles and a slightly larger, purple cone, with no prickles. They both have 5 needles and exhibit the slight Krumholz effect of wind. But on the mesa, I think the Whitebark pines were taller, straighter.

A LIST OF BIRDS HEARD OR SEEN FROM WHITNEY PORTAL TO TULAINYO LAKE OVERLOOK
on June 27-28 2000
(in approximate phylogenetic order)

American Kestrel
Blue Grouse
Mountain Quail
Rufous Hummingbird (a migrant)
Northern Flicker
Red-naped Sapsucker
Steller's Jay
Clark's Nutcracker
Common Raven
Mountain Chickadee
White-breasted Nuthatch
American Dipper
Swainson's Thrush
American Robin
Townsend's Solitaire
American Pipit
Yellow-rumped Warbler
Dark-eye Junco
Grey-crowned Rosy-Finch
Cassin's Finch

Golden-crowned Kinglet (October 3, 2000)

• •

APPENDIX E

CONGRESSIONAL RECORD
OF THE
UNITED STATES OF AMERICA

VOL. 144, NO. 143
WASHINGTON, MONDAY, OCTOBER 12, 1998

House of Representatives

CELEBRATING THE RICH HISTORY OF MT. WHITNEY

HON. JERRY LEWIS
OF CALIFORNIA
IN THE HOUSE OF REPRESENTATIVES
Monday, October 12, 1998

Mr. Speaker, I would like to bring to your attention today the 125th anniversary of the first ascent of Mt. Whitney, the highest mountain peak in the continental United States at 14,494 feet, located in California's Inyo County.

In the early 1870's, as the Owens Valley community first began to attract settlers, local residents often visited nearby Soda Springs to fish, hunt, and to escape the summer heat. In August of 1873, a large group of Lone Pine locals were camping in this area when three of them decided to take a hike up to the summit. Previous attempts to climb this mountain had been made by Clarence King, in party with a California Geological Survey expedition sponsored by Josiah Whitney. King identified the mountain and named it "Mount Whitney" in 1864. He claimed to have reached the summit in 1871, but it was soon discovered that he missed the mark and accidentally climbed another peak.

The "Three Fishermen" (locals Charley Begole, Johnny Lucas and Al Johnson) credited with Whitney's first ascent made the hike from Soda Springs to the summit and back in one day on August 18, 1873. They christened the mountain "Fishermen's Peak," which touched off a controversy that lasted several years. The Lone Pine residents were not in favor of the name "Mount Whitney," since they did not share a high opinion of Mr. Whitney. Local residents petitioned in favor of the names "Fishermen's Peak," "Fowler's Peak," or "Dome of Inyo," anything but "Mount Whitney," which is the name that stands today.

Undaunted by the unwanted name, local residents raised funds and built a trail to the summit in 1904. Mr. Gustave F. Marsh of Lone Pine was the engineer who led this effort. He also served as contractor and supervisor for the Smithsonian Institute in 1909 when the trail was repaired and the summit shelter was built. Local residents again pitched in to raise funds for this effort. The summit hut was originally financed by the Smithsonian for astronomical and atmospheric research purposes.

The early residents of the region were largely farmers and miners. As the trail and hut stand today, no one really knows how many hundreds of thousands of people from all walks of life and from all countries of the world have climbed to the summit of Mount Whitney. Also, very little has ever been mentioned of the Native Americans, who knew of the peak and in their world, called it "The Old One," or "The High One."

On August 18, 1998, as a tribute to these early settlers, another group of local residents climbed Mount Whitney to pay honor to the contribution made by these pioneers. Several descendants of the original group still live in the Lone Pine area.

I can well remember donning a backpack and sleeping bag and hitting the trail with Hulda Crooks, better known on the mountain as Grandma Whitney, in August, 1986. A friendship was born over those days that has been among the most special and enduring of my life. Because of her legacy, Congress passed legislation and Hulda returned to Mt. Whitney in 1991 for the announcement that Crooks Peak, adjacent to the Whitney summit, would forever bear her name. Hulda was a mentor and teacher an remained one of my dearest friends over the years until her passing last November.

Mr. Speaker, I ask that you join me and our colleagues in paying tribute to the men and women who have provided Mt. Whitney with its rich and textured history. Without any question, for every person who has ever climbed or tried to climb this magnificent peak, Mt. Whitney holds its own special memories, and its own meaningful place in their life.

Mount Whitney (photo by Wm Ross)

•••••••••••••••••••••••••••

APPENDIX F

"TIMELESS MOUNTAIN"
by
Elisabeth Newbold and Doug Thompson
Published in a special Millennium Edition
of the
Inyo Register
November 25, 1999

"...escape to the mountain, lest thou be consumed."
(Genesis 19:17)

We stand before the mileage sign of the New Millennium, pondering time and how it changes things. The past 1,000 years have engraved dramatic alterations upon many features of our planet. Some, however, stand impervious.

Today, "web cams" broadcast rapidly changing images of weather, waves, and landscapes worldwide. But if we had an archive containing clips of Mount Whitney shot every month for the past 1,000 years (a total of 12,000 shots) the changes would barely be perceptible.

If greatly enlarged, the last 150 frames might reveal evidence of humans on the horizon: a trail in the making, a hut on the summit, bonfires signaling visits to the top. Let's focus in, and sift through the last 100-plus years of events at Mount Whitney:

* First Ascent: August 18, 1873, 126 years ago. It was a group of three men who first stood on the summit--fishing buddies from Lone Pine. Previous attempts by Clarence King had failed. Charley Begole, Johnny Lucas, and Al Johnson

241

carved their names in history one summer day, when they climbed the mountain on an impulse. Locals dubbed it "Fisherman's Peak," but the official name became "Mount Whitney," named after Josiah Whitney, Professor at the California Academy of Sciences and founder of the California Geological Survey.

* First Overnight Stay on Top: September 2-3, 1881, 118 years ago. Summer was drawing to a close when Captain Otho E. Michaelis, along with two or three others of his party, hauled a tent and a quarter-cord of wood to the top. The wind was so fierce they could not put up the tent, and their campfire consumed all of their wood long before the sun came up. Like many others since, they did not get any sleep during their cold night on the summit of Mount Whitney.

* Completion of Mt. Whitney Trail: July 17, 1904, 95 years ago. The trail was begun in 1903, but efforts fizzled as supplies ran out. The people of Inyo County rallied to support the project, raised $200, and contracted Gustave F. Marsh to take over the effort. Enduring cold, wind, and snow until the end of October, Marsh and his small crew were disappointed to leave the trail unfinished. During the winter, fund-raising activities yielded enough to support renewed efforts the following season. From *"The Highest House"* printed in the San Francisco Chronicle, Sunday, Nov. 7, 1909:

"When within but a few hundred yards of the summit they came upon a chasm which it seemed no human foot could cross. 'We're done beat now for sure,' the men groaned when they behold the precipitous cliff, but Marsh only smiled and set the dynamite to work reducing the angle of the cliff until the gap was bridged with debris. At last, on the 17th of July, the builders of the trail had finished their work and with a cheer the first pack train trampled the flat roof of Whitney."

* Completion of Summit Shelter: August 27, 1909, 90 years ago. The Smithsonian Institution contracted Mr. Marsh to build the summit shelter. The trail needed repair before this could be accomplished. Marsh and his crew suffered snow blindness, altitude sickness, and limited resources. It took until July 28 to reestablish the trail and lead the first pack train to the summit. Work quickly commenced on the stone hut. As it took shape, a violent thunderstorm drove all but Marsh into desertion. He resolved to finish the hut if he had to do it by himself. Thanks to his tenacity, the others returned a few days later. The shelter was completed two days early, and $250 under budget. Dr. Charles Abbot, Director of the Smithsonian Astrophysical Observatory, wrote that Marsh "will never get paid in this world for the work he did on that house," which included cooking, carrying stone and snow, riveting and cementing, as well as "general bossing."

* Visit of Halley's comet: May 23, 1910, 89 years ago. Again we turn to Gustave Marsh for another "freeze frame" in Mount Whitney's recent history. Marsh climbed the peak alone to watch the sky show: a total lunar eclipse plus the comet. "...The moon came up full speed ... for the first quarter of the moon it was cloudy but after that it was clear. The comet was in plain view as soon as it was dark ... [it] showed up grand and was in plain sight until the head ... got in the fog bank. It seemed particularly bright at about 8:30 ... when the moon was almost covered. The tail almost reached the moon. It swept almost across the sky. I feel I had the best view of anyone outside of an observatory." (G. F. Marsh, Letter to Prof. W. W. Campbell, June 5, 1910)

* First Airplane Flight over Whitney Summit: 1914, 85 years ago. Residents of Inyo, Mono and Alpine counties joined together to promote attention to the Owens Valley. The Inyo

Good Road Club organized and publicized this event, which took place during Aviation Week. Silas Christofferson flew a tractor biplane over the Whitney summit on the morning of June 25, setting a new altitude record for flight: 15,725 feet. Powered by a 100 HP engine, the plane weight a total of 1,850 pounds, including the pilot, one passenger, and 30 gallons of gas.

* Construction of Road, Pond, Campgrounds: 1933-35, 64 years ago. As more people came to visit Mount Whitney, more accommodations were built. The original Whitney Portal Road was constructed in 1933-35, making it possible for tourists to drive their automobiles up from Lone Pine into the lush little canyon. The original route followed the early pack trail, and a small part of it can be seen today below the existing road, an area known in the past as "Hunter's Flat." Public campgrounds, picnic areas, and a fishing pond were built by the post-depression Civilian Conservation Corps (CCC), with the U.S. Forest Service, to enhance the region. The Forest Service maintained the public areas until recently, when some services were sub-contracted out. Most visitors are not aware of the work behind the scenes. It is the time and effort of both paid employees and volunteers that keep the road clear, the trees healthy, the bathrooms clean, and the trash removed.

* "Wedding of the Waters" Event: 1935, 64 years ago. Father John J. Crowley was much more to Inyo County than a Catholic priest. He adopted the entire community and was beloved by many people of all denominations. His vision included growth and prosperity for the area, and he used his flair for public relations to stage this press event. Indian runners filled a gourd with pure, icy water from the nation's highest lake (Lake Tulainyo) just north of Mount Whitney's summit. The gourd was transported in turn by pony express, burro, covered

wagon, mule team, railroad car, and airplane. Finally, it was sprinkled from the plane into Badwater in Death Valley, the lowest body of water in the U.S. News of this fascinating ceremony spread all over California and beyond, focusing widespread attention on the region.

* Construction of Whitney Portal Store: 1935, 64 years ago. The Whitney Portal Store and pack station was built in 1935. It has changed hands several times, and it is hard to find a long-time local who hasn't cooked hamburgers at the Store or worked on pack trips.

* Construction of Cabins: 1935-1950, 50 years ago. The private cabin lots were each claimed and developed individually. These summer homes were built over a period of 16 years. Their varying sizes, styles, and decor attest to each one's unique design. One cabin burned down in 1950, and was rebuilt. Two more suffered serious damage in the great storms of 1969. That memorable winter was a harsh reminder of what nature can do when its full power is unleashed in the Eastern Sierra.

* Passage of Wilderness Act: 1964, 34 years ago. The heavy traffic through Whitney Portal and on the Whitney Trail took its toll. Concern about preserving the natural habitat led to adding the Whitney area to the Wilderness Act in 1964. This put strict limitations on the area--no mechanical equipment or new buildings, with very few exceptions.

* Ban of Pack Animals, Use of Trail Permits: 1970's, 25 years ago. In a continued effort to limit the impact on visitors on the Whitney Trail, the Forest Service banned pack animals in the 1970's. While horses, mules, and even llamas are still used in other areas of the back country for transporting equipment and supplies, they are no longer allowed on Mount Whitney. A quote system was put into place, requiring overnight permits.

* Regrowth of Outpost Camp, Mirror Lake: 1980's, 15

years ago. With pack animals no longer on the Whitney Trail, and foot traffic somewhat reduced by the quota system, meadows and other grassy areas had a chance to recover from overuse. The large, flat area now known as Outpost Camp (or Bighorn Sheep Park) had suffered from the annual trampling and grazing. The fragile section around Mirror Lake was also damaged. These areas experienced dramatic regrowth during the 1980's, and are once again lush with vegetation.

* Use of bear boxes, cell phones, web pages: 1990's, 5 years ago. One would expect that bear sightings might be less frequent than they were 100 years ago, but the Whitney Portal bears have adapted to the 1990's by losing their fear of man and developing a taste for junk food. Widespread damage to parked cars containing food has led to the installation of bear-proof containers at the Whitney Portal campgrounds. Other new developments include information access on the Internet, and the common use of digital/wireless telephones. Recently, a message was posted on the Whitney Portal Store's web site (www.395.com/portal) by a hiker who observed he was the only one on the summit without a cell phone. In contrast, Gustave Marsh (in 1909) signaled his wife in Lone Pine with a mirror by day and a bonfire by night. Technology has exploded in the last decade, offering intriguing new toys for the backpacker. Instead of a compass and map, one can own a personal GPS (global positioning system). Instead of a journal, one can type the daily log into a palmtop computer.

Returning our focus to the wide angle lens, all this change is a mere pebble on the rocky granite buttresses that loom above us as we scan the horizon of Mount Whitney. When we stand back and think about it, nothing much about this landmark has really changed. A comfortable presence, it keeps its timeless watch over the surrounding peaks and valleys.

Those of us who are close neighbors of Mount Whitney need to remember its global significance. Thousands of visitors from all over the world have passed through Whitney Portal. The history of the mountain was important enough to elicit an entry in the U.S. Congressional Record last year.

The Mountain is still there. People still sense the need to climb it--to reach for something higher. However, what you may see nowadays, from the 360-degree view on the summit, is a degradation of air quality in all directions. Sometimes the Whitney drainage is so covered with dust from Owens Lake, you can't see the mountain. The frequent noise from low-flying aircraft distracts from the natural experience of hiking the trail. While Mount Whitney stands stalwart, the encroachments of nearby communities threaten its sanctity. As areas alongside of the wilderness develop, the impact tends to spill over. Thus, measures taken in neighboring cities--even several hundred miles away--may affect the quality of the Mount Whitney wilderness experience more than what is done locally. Perhaps this should be the focus of the next 100 years.

Max & Elisabeth Newbold on the mountain with Doug Sr.
(photo by Sally Anderson)

Order Form

To Order Additional Copies of

Mount Whitney:
Mountain Lore From the Whitney Store

Mail this form to:

Westwind Publishing Company
548 N. Westwind Drive
El Cajon, CA 92020

Name: _____

Mailing Address: _____

City/State/Zip/Country: _____

___ copies @ $14.95 each   Subtotal $_____

Shipping/handling (U.S. Priority Mail)
    $4.00 first copy, $1.00 each add'l $_____

CA residents add .075% sales tax $_____

                            TOTAL $_____

Make check or money order payable to
Westwind Publishing Company

OR, order online at www.whitneyportalstore.com